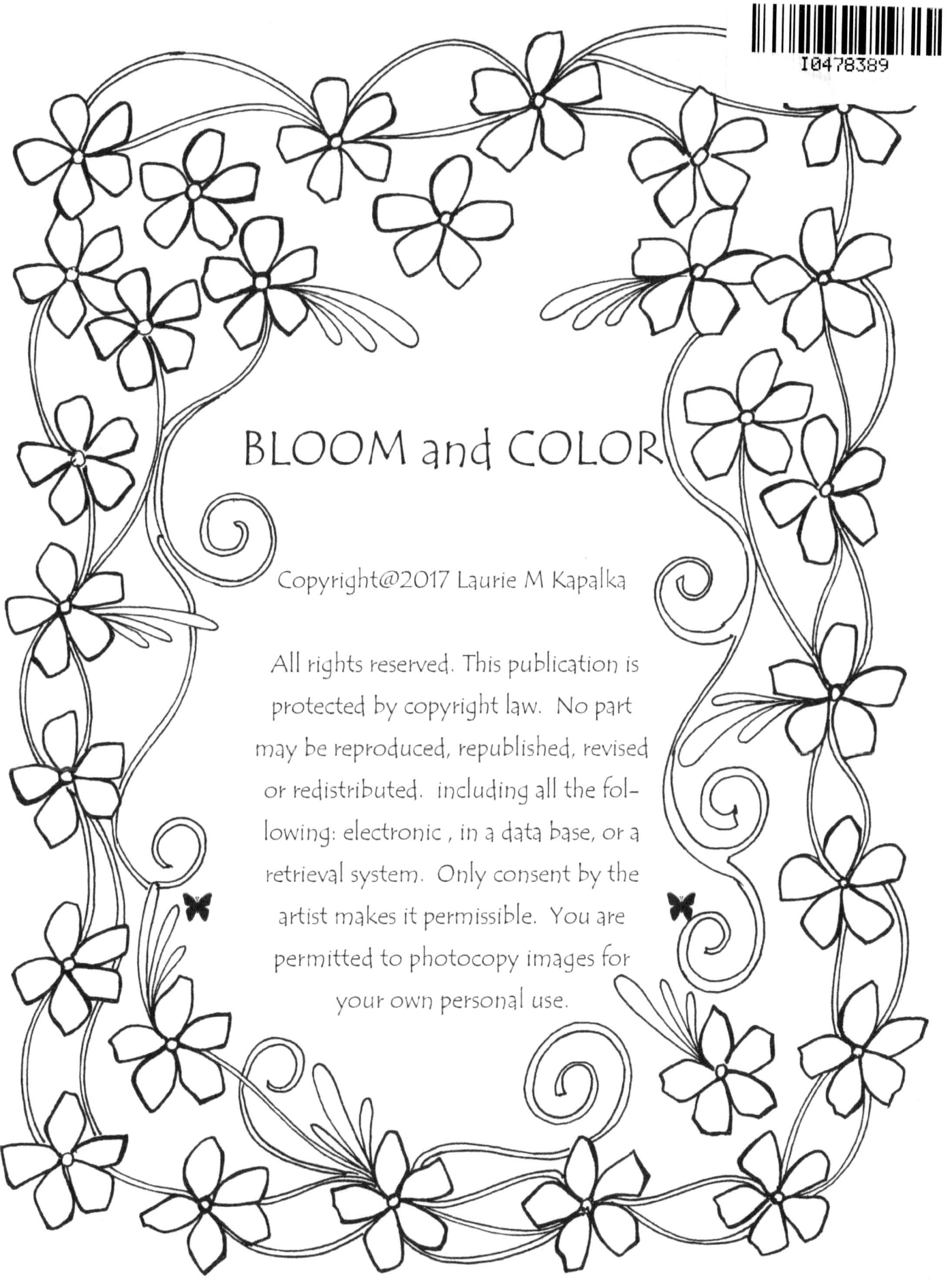

BLOOM and COLOR

Copyright@2017 Laurie M Kapalka

All rights reserved. This publication is
protected by copyright law. No part
may be reproduced, republished, revised
or redistributed. including all the fol-
lowing: electronic , in a data base, or a
retrieval system. Only consent by the
artist makes it permissible. You are
permitted to photocopy images for
your own personal use.

I0478389

Never quit blooming

Sunshine glistened on her face
and the smell of sweet flowers filled the air
as she tended her garden
with love and with care

The array of colors
thriving in beauty
kept blossoming and blossoming
and never quit blooming

Her bright cheerful ways
and peaceful nature
brought hope and love to all
that had met her

Although words can never describe
her true beauty
her memory remains
like a delicate flower
that never quit blooming

In memory of my sweet mom Nettie
I will love you forever

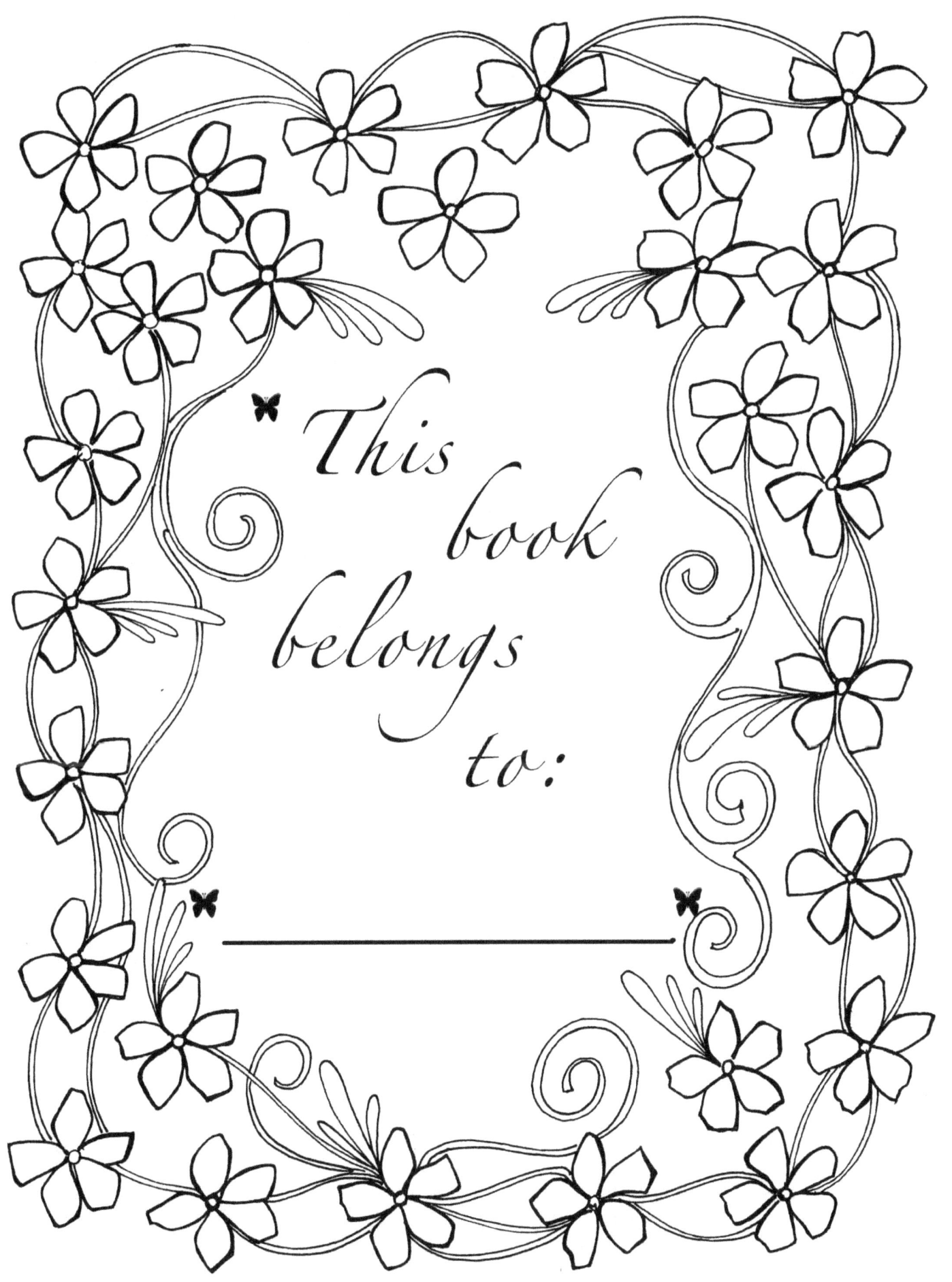

This book belongs to:

_____

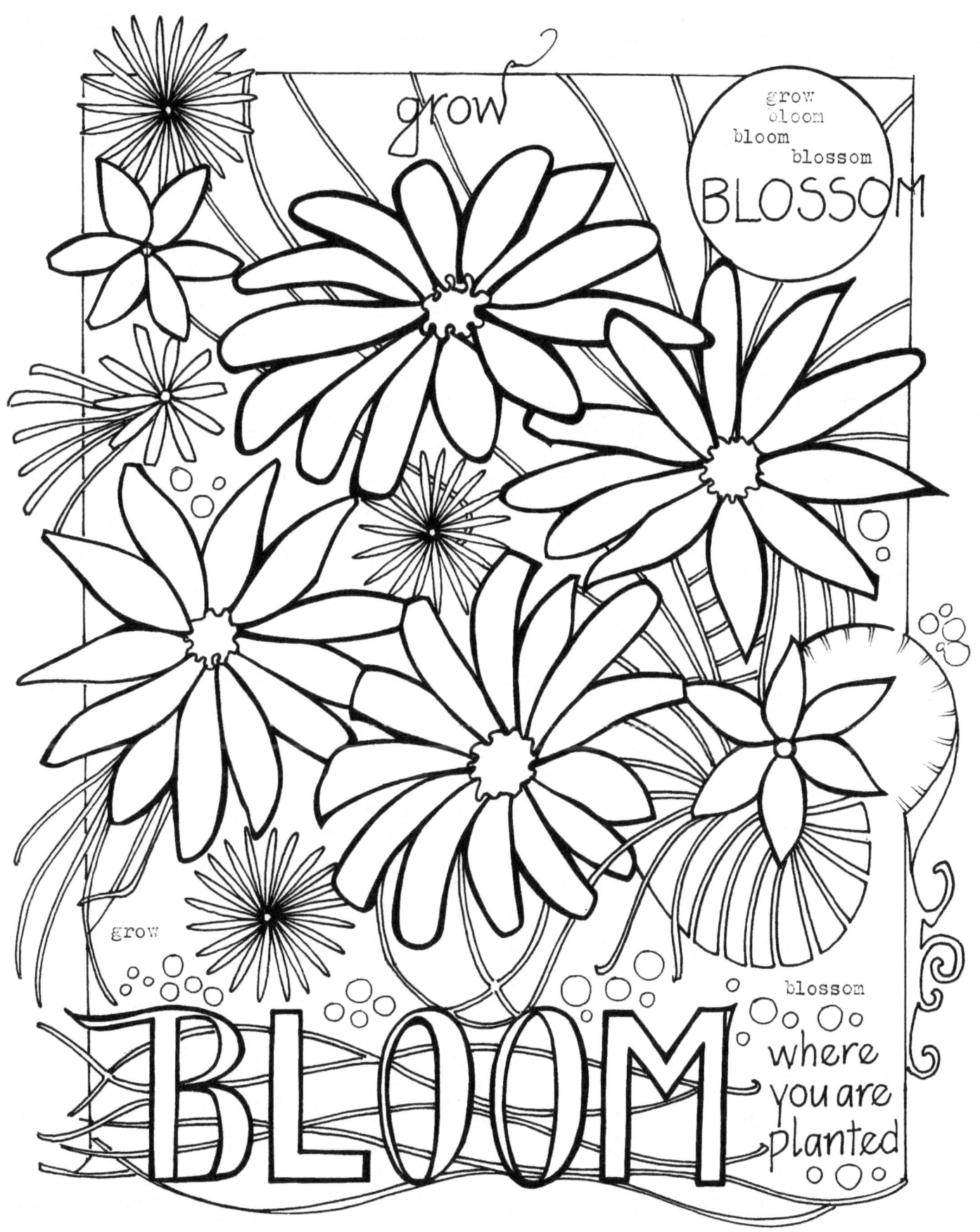

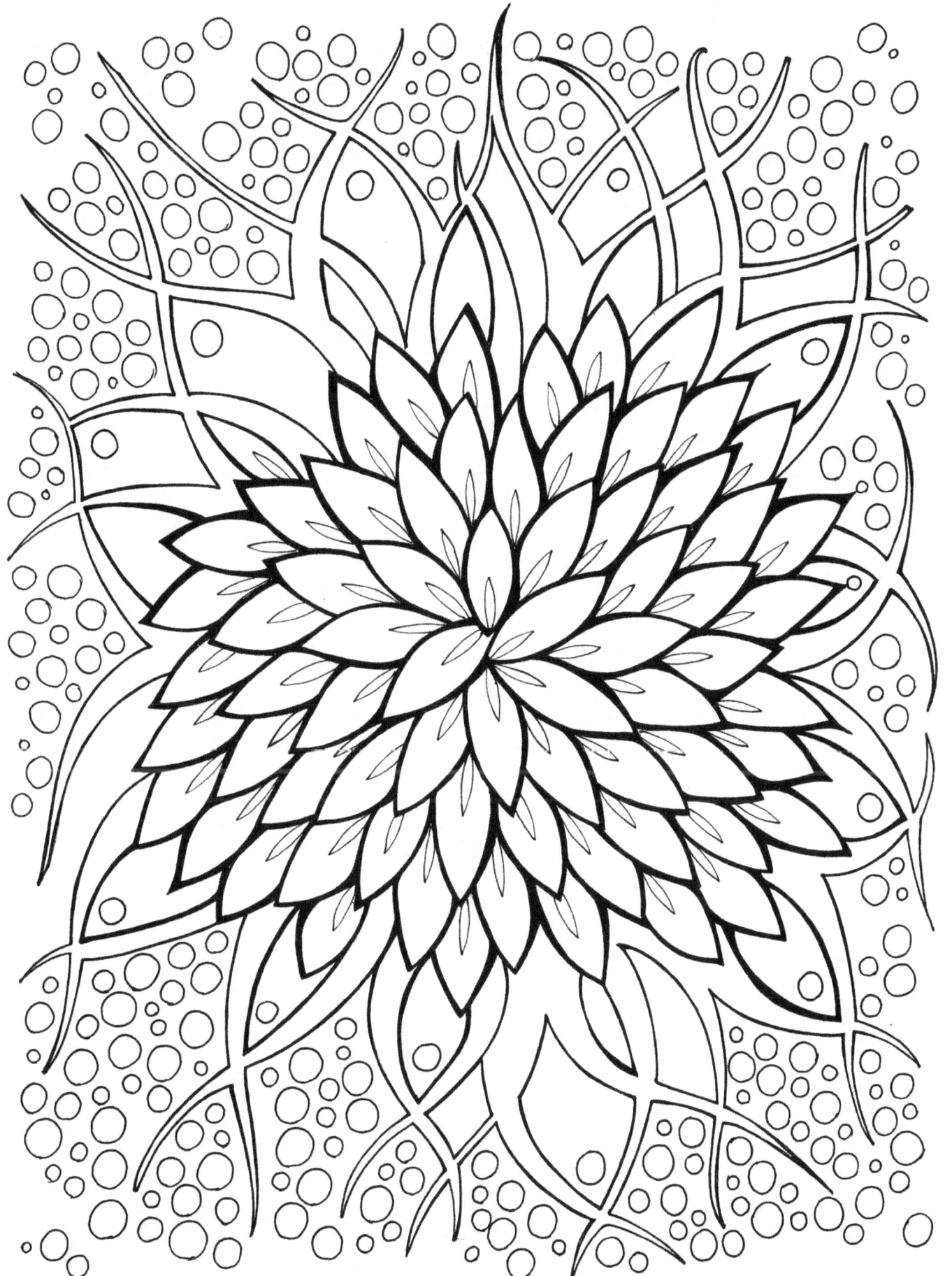

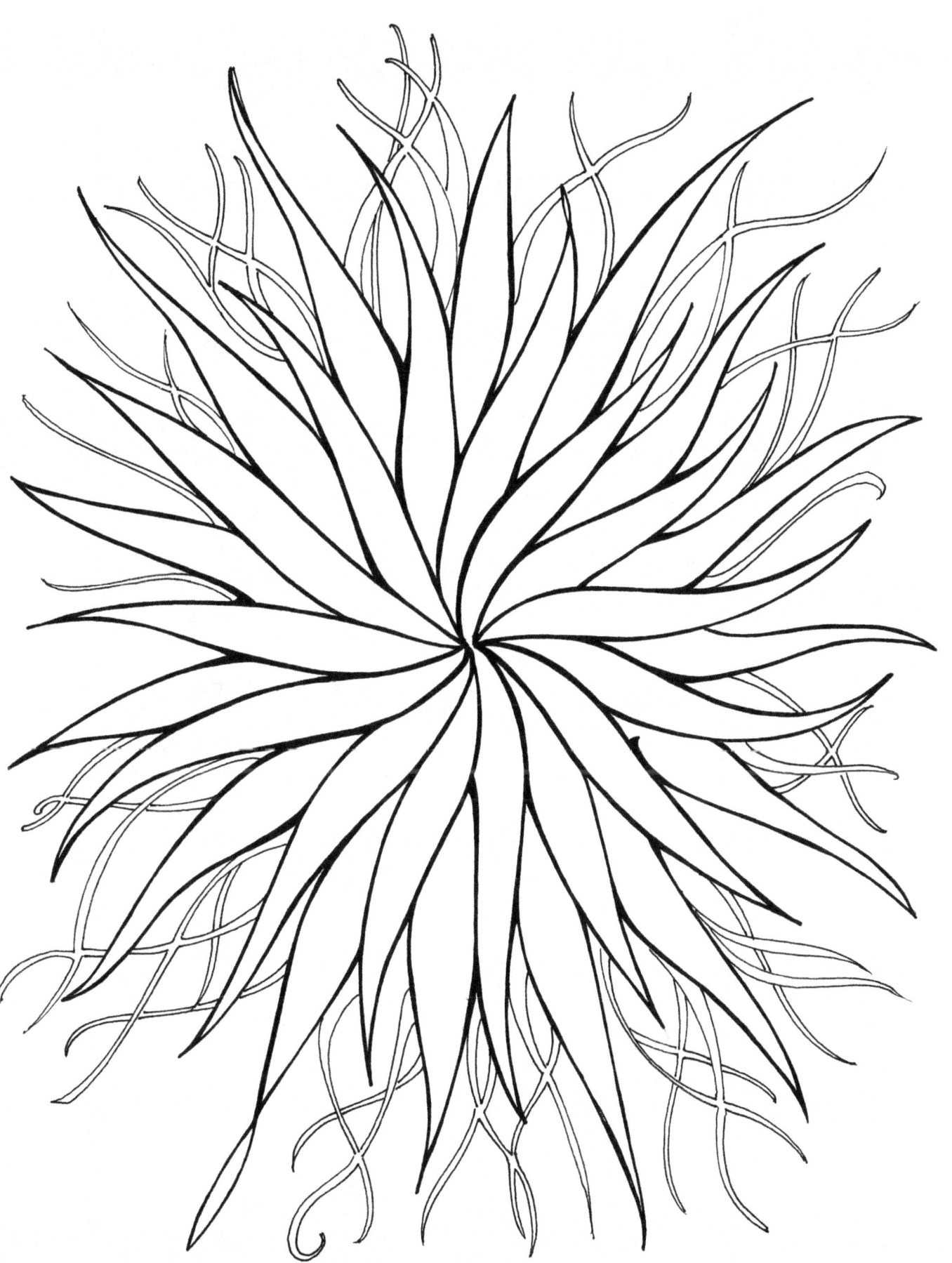

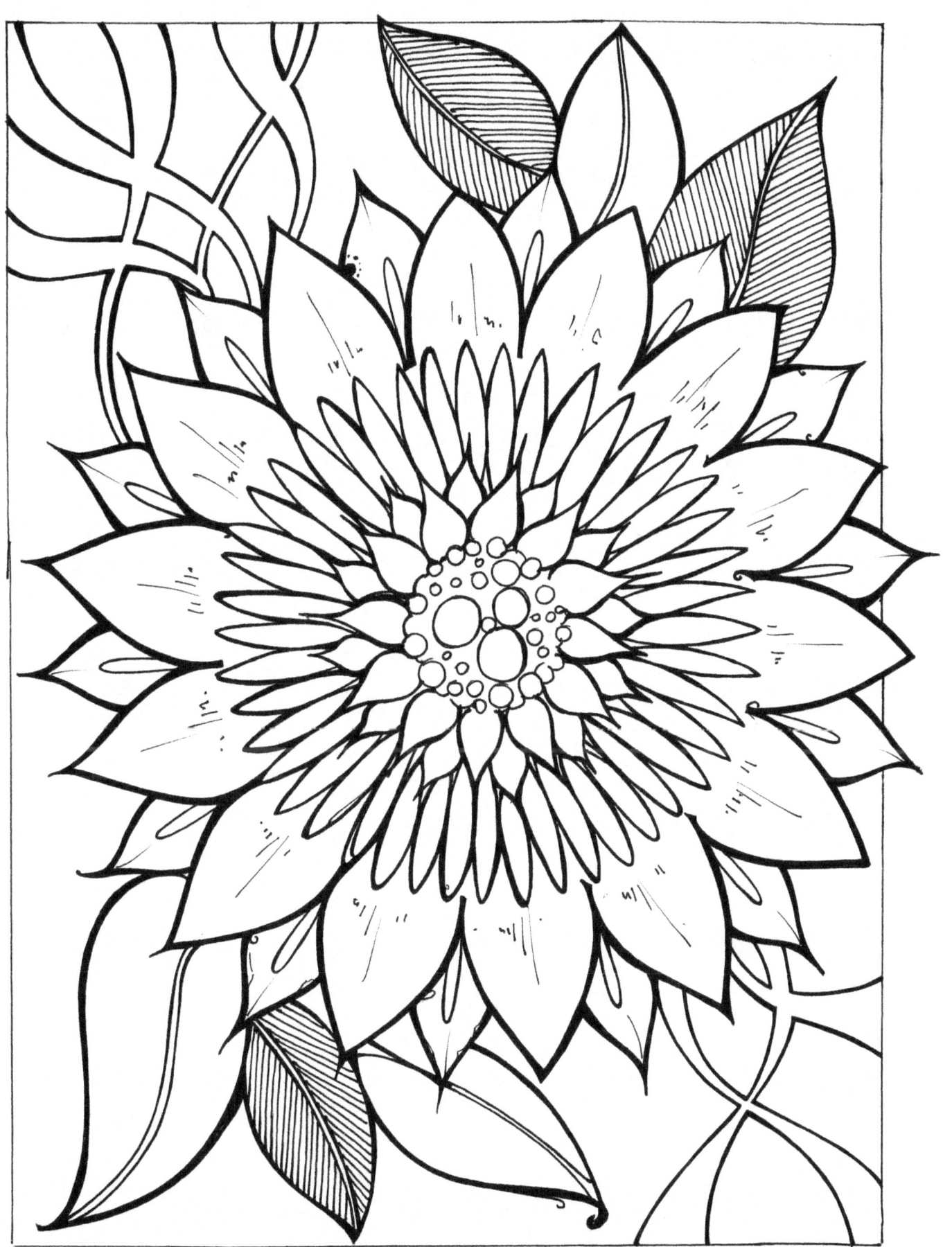

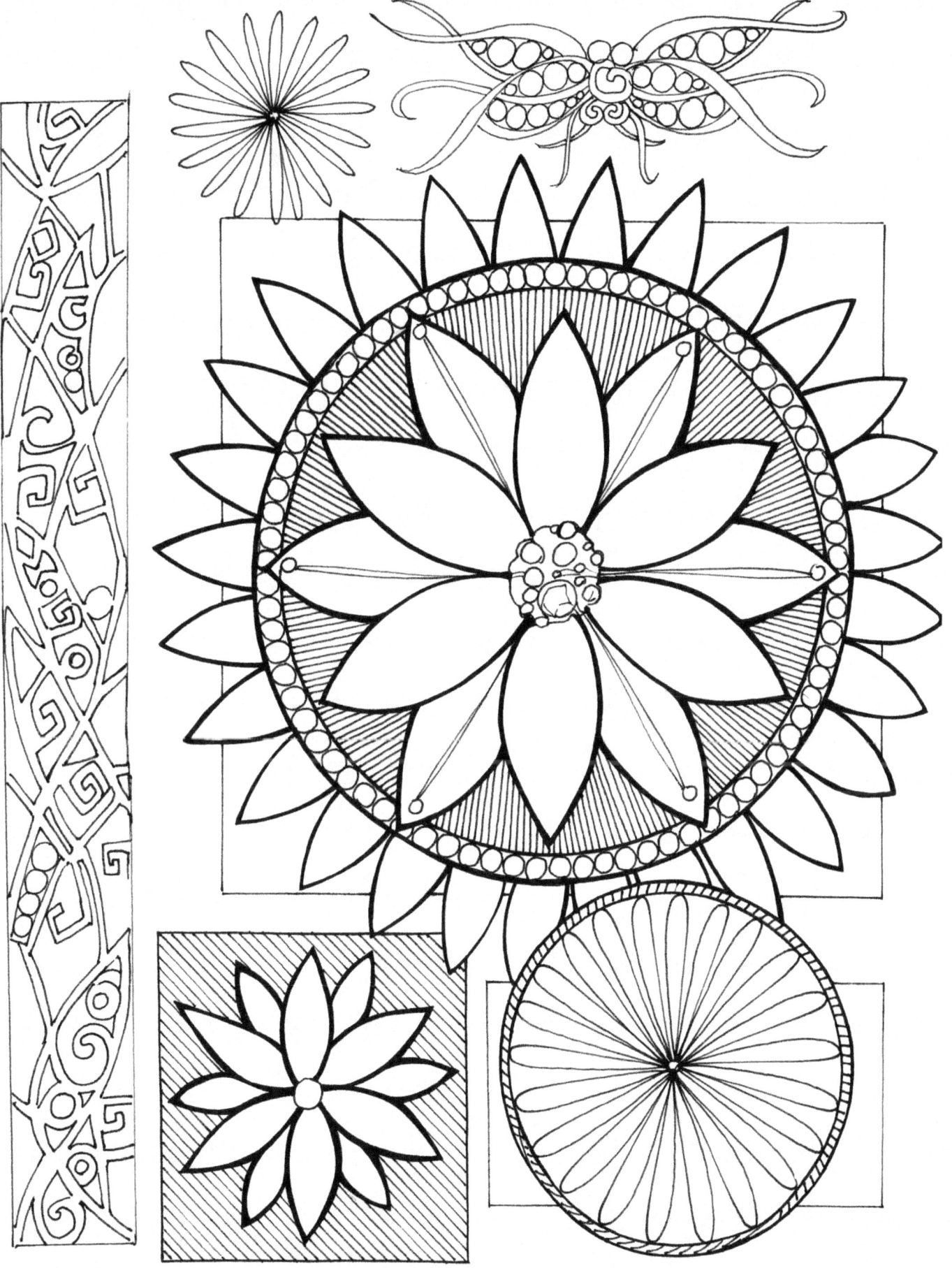

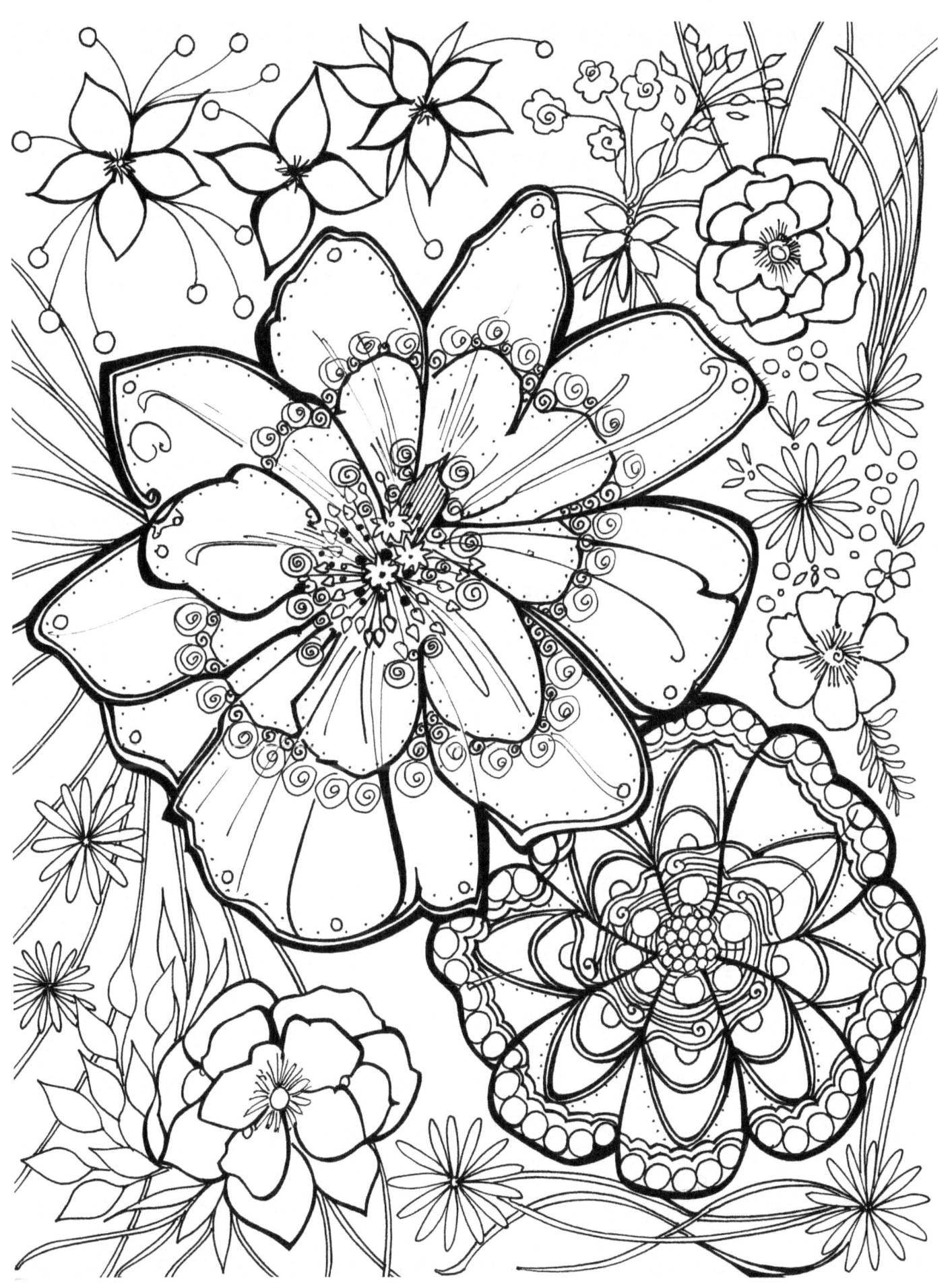

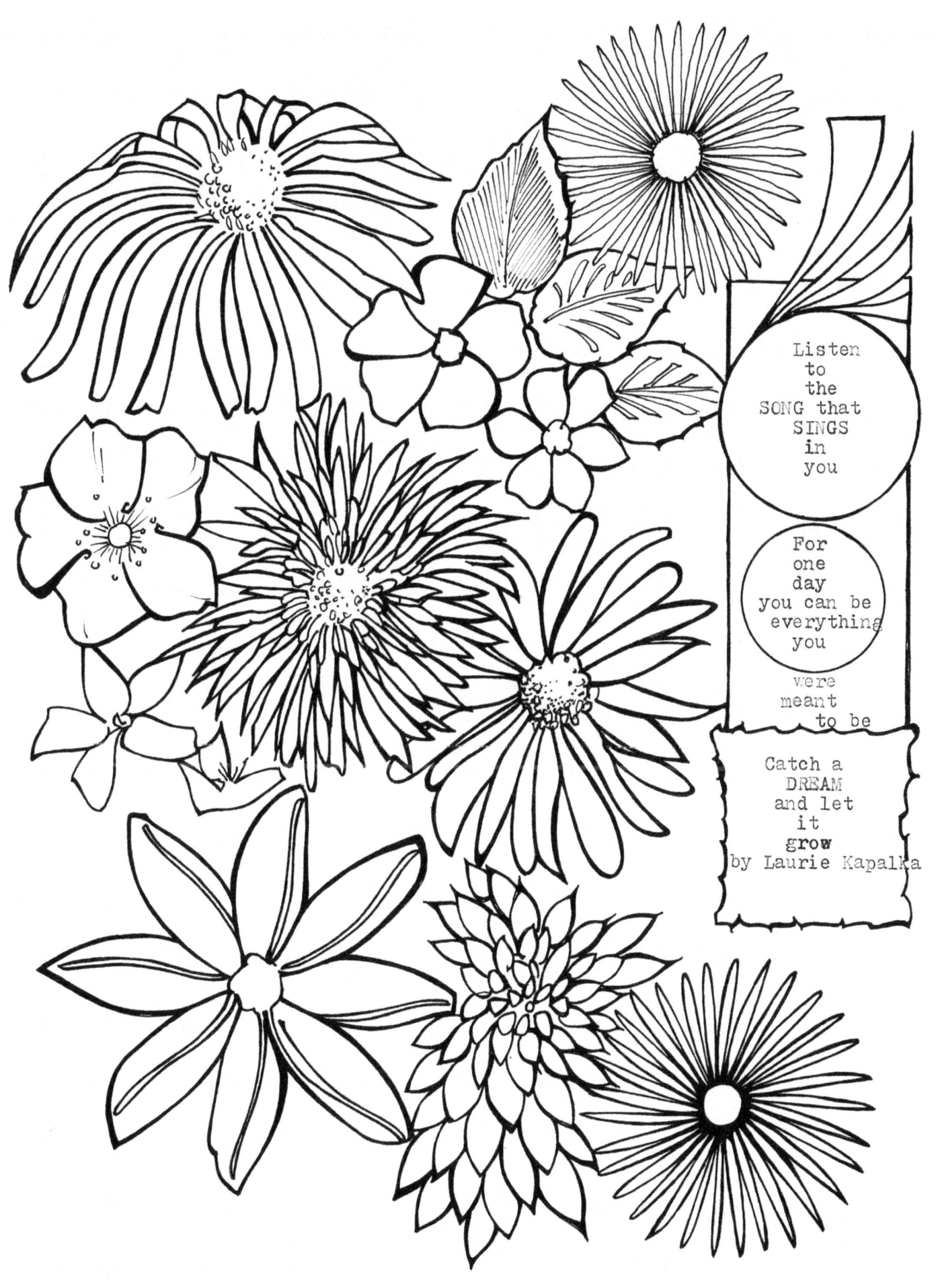

Listen
to
the
SONG that
SINGS
in
you

For
one
day
you can be
everything
you

were
meant
to be

Catch a
DREAM
and let
it
grow
by Laurie Kapalka

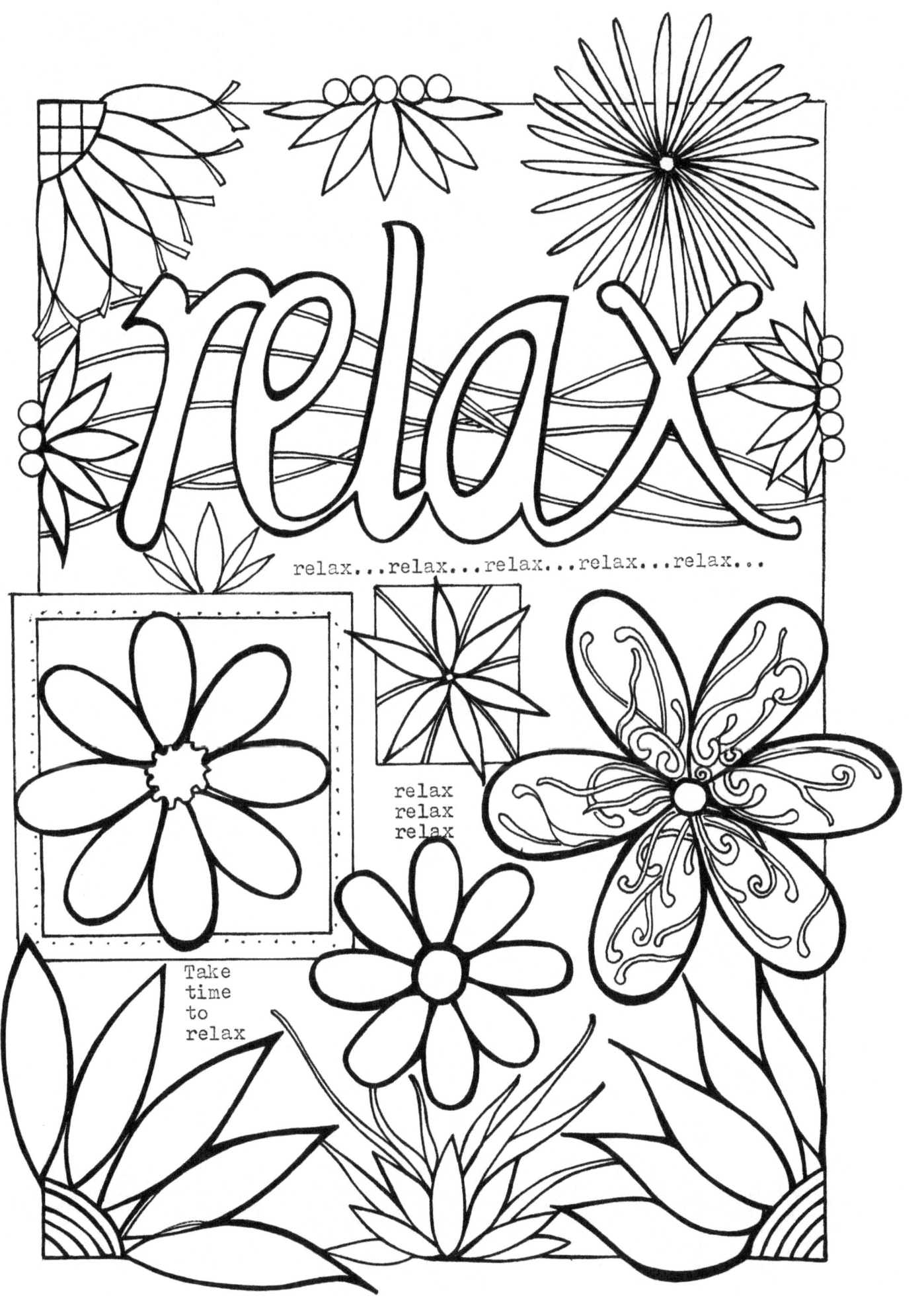

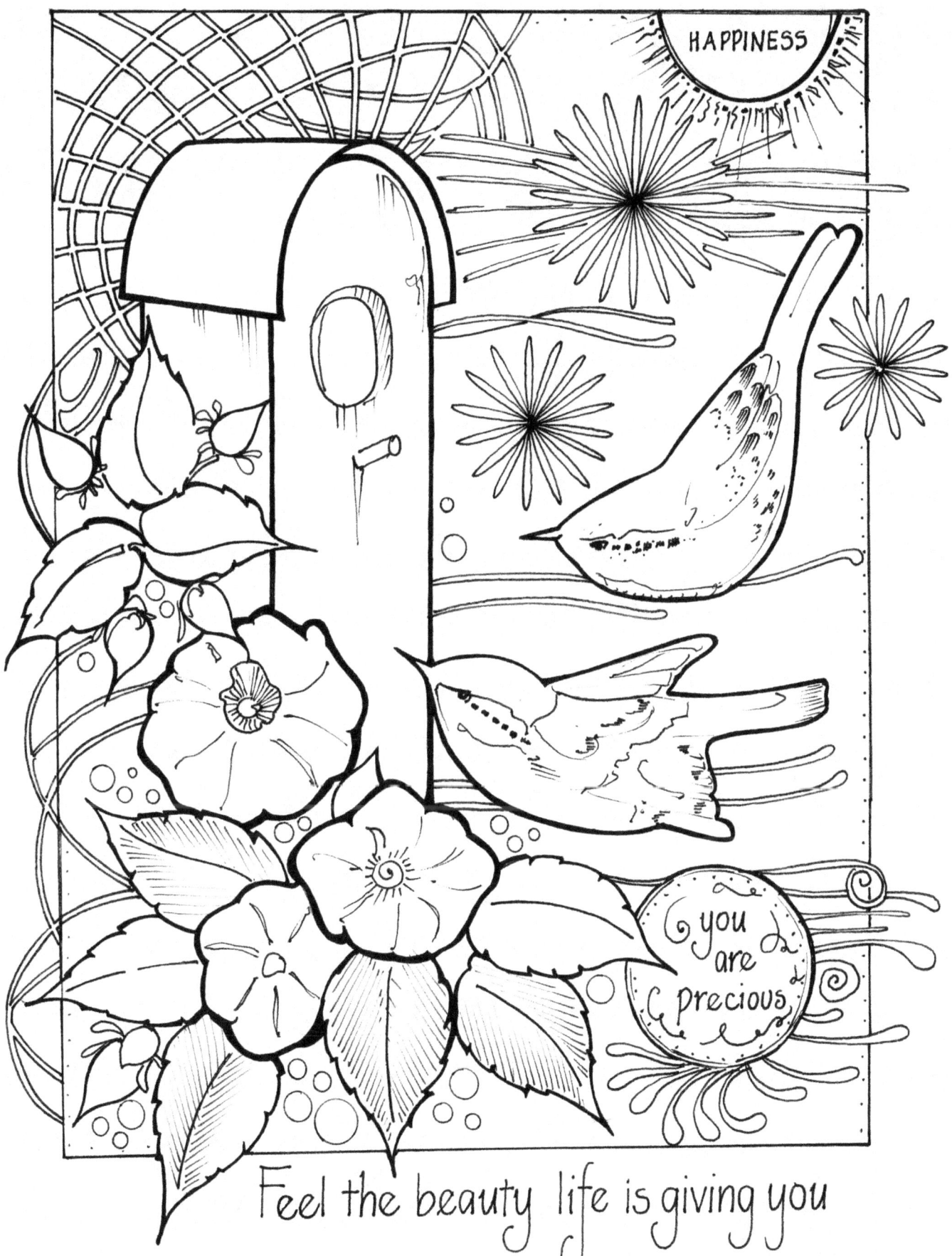

Feel the beauty life is giving you

I would rather have one little rose from the garden of a
friend than the choicest flower when my stay on earth must
end.

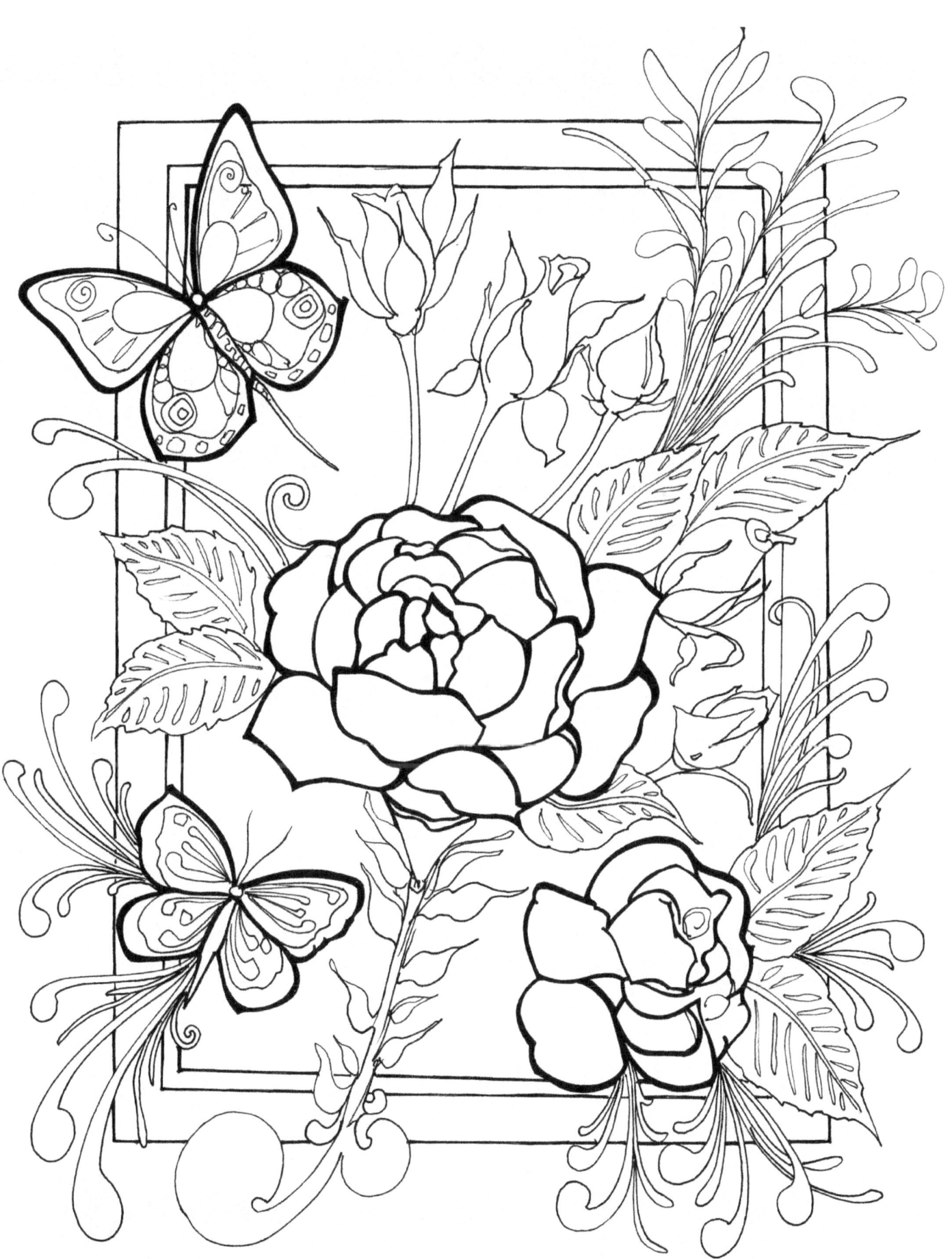

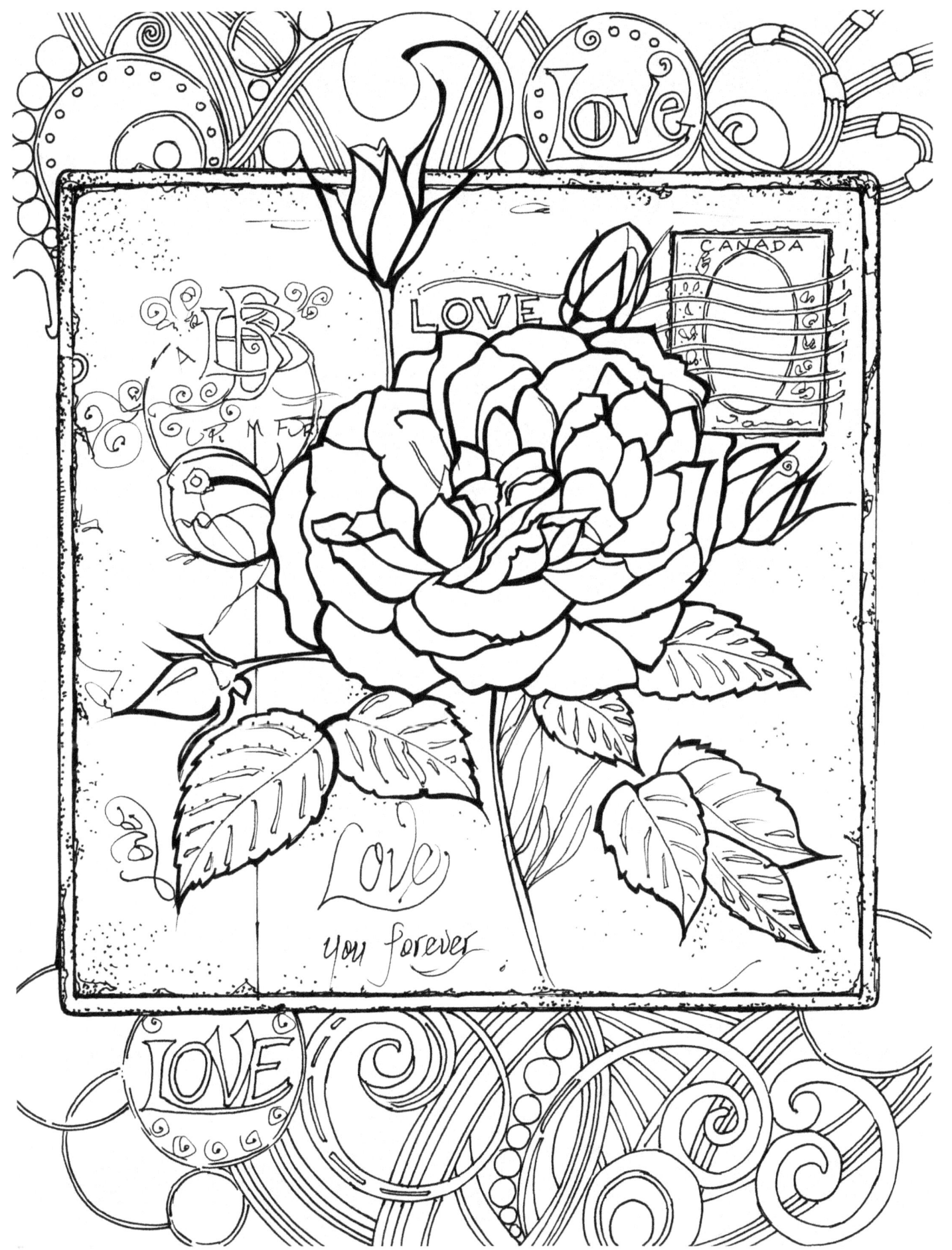

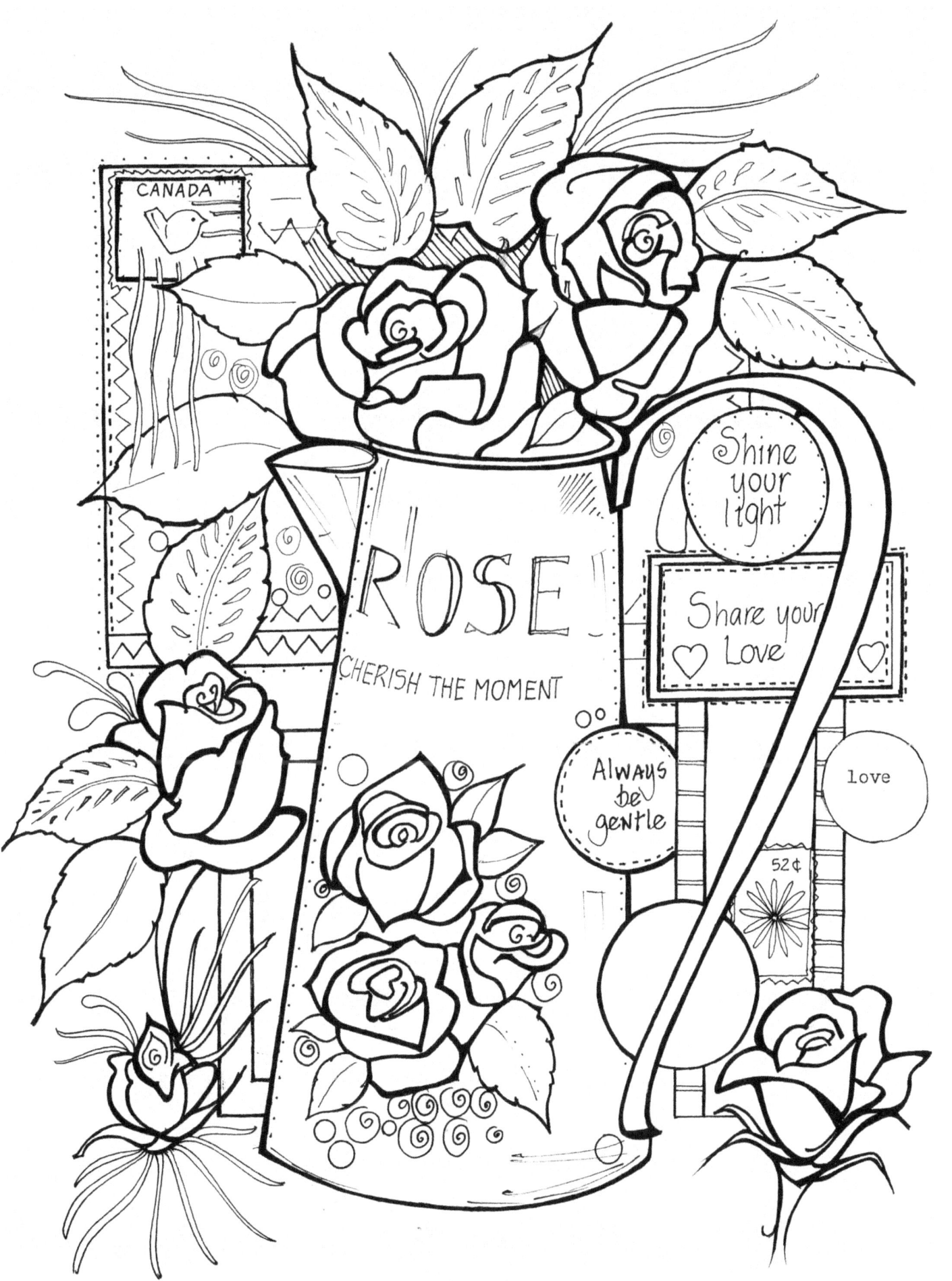

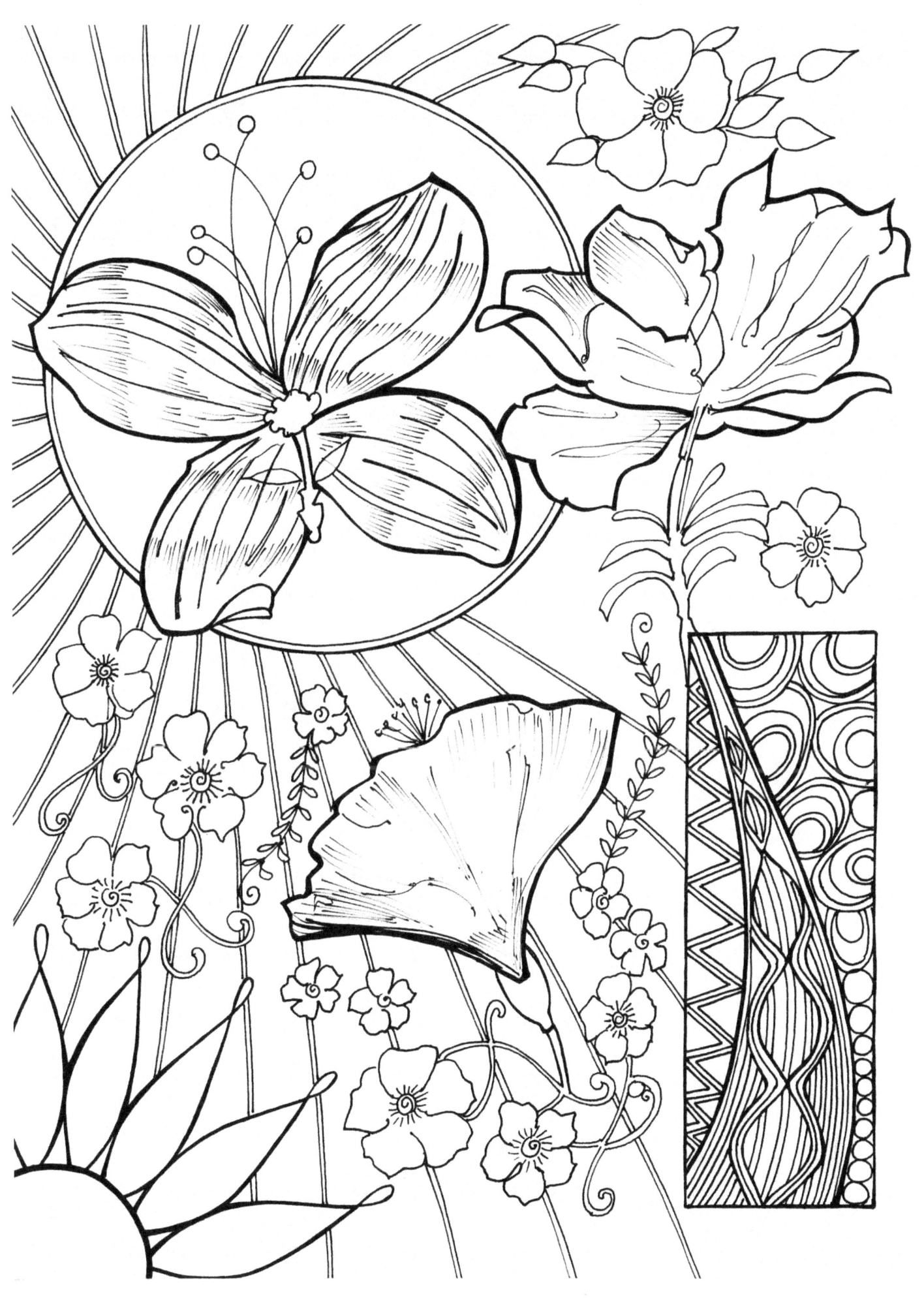

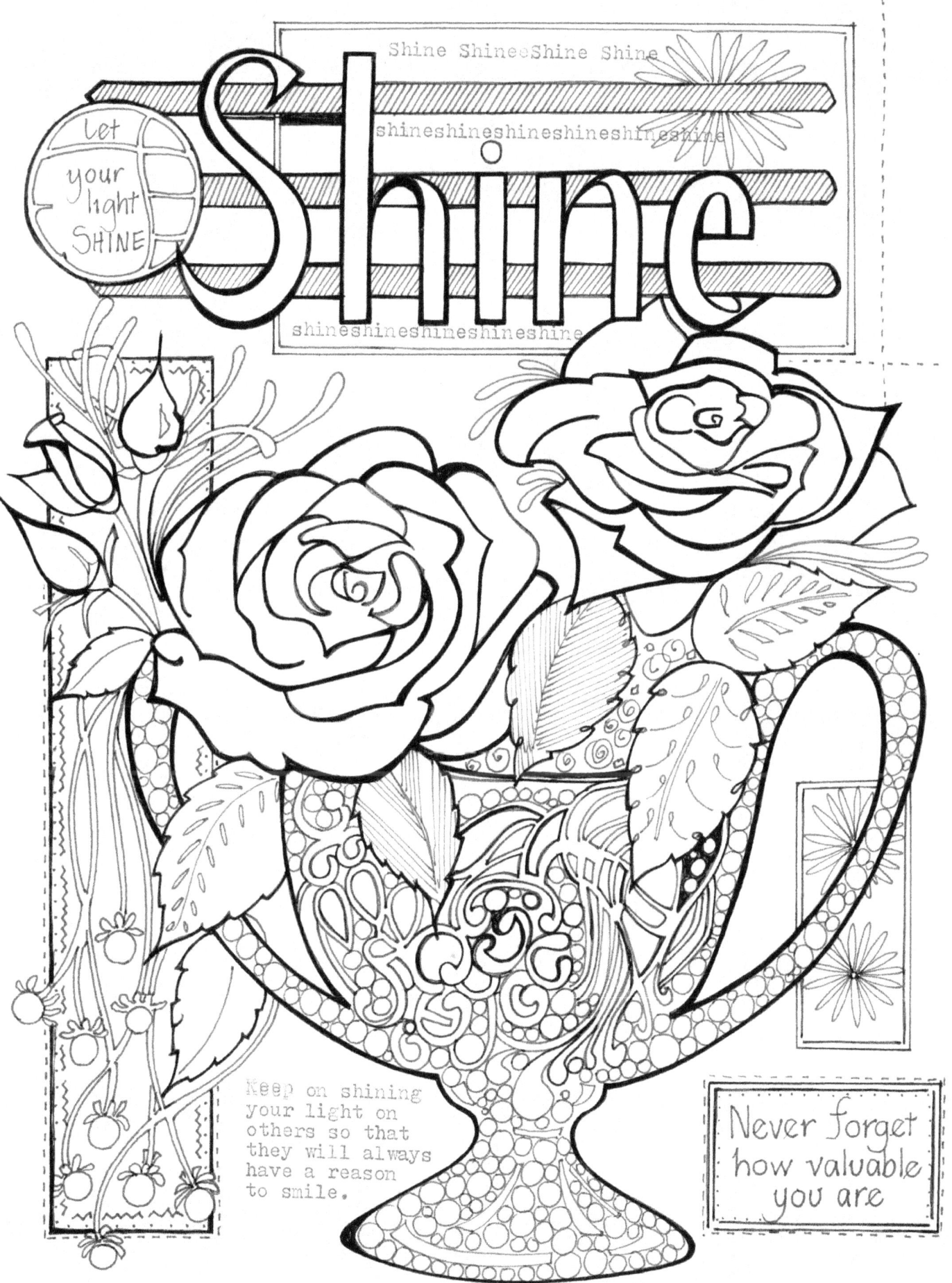

Let your light SHINE

Shine ShineeShine Shine
shineshineshineshineshineshine
Shine
shineshineshineshineshine

Keep on shining
your light on
others so that
they will always
have a reason
to smile.

Never forget
how valuable
you are

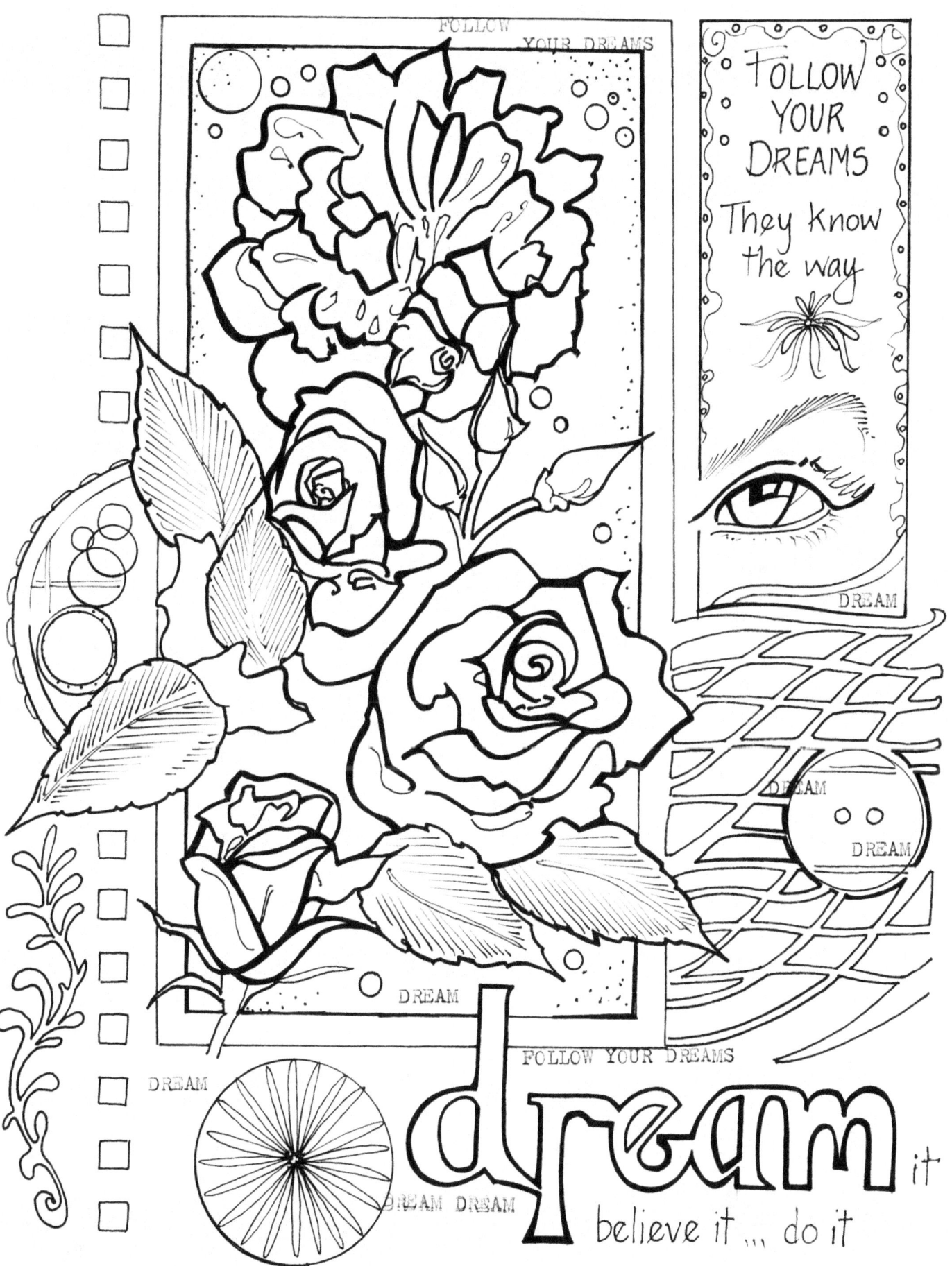

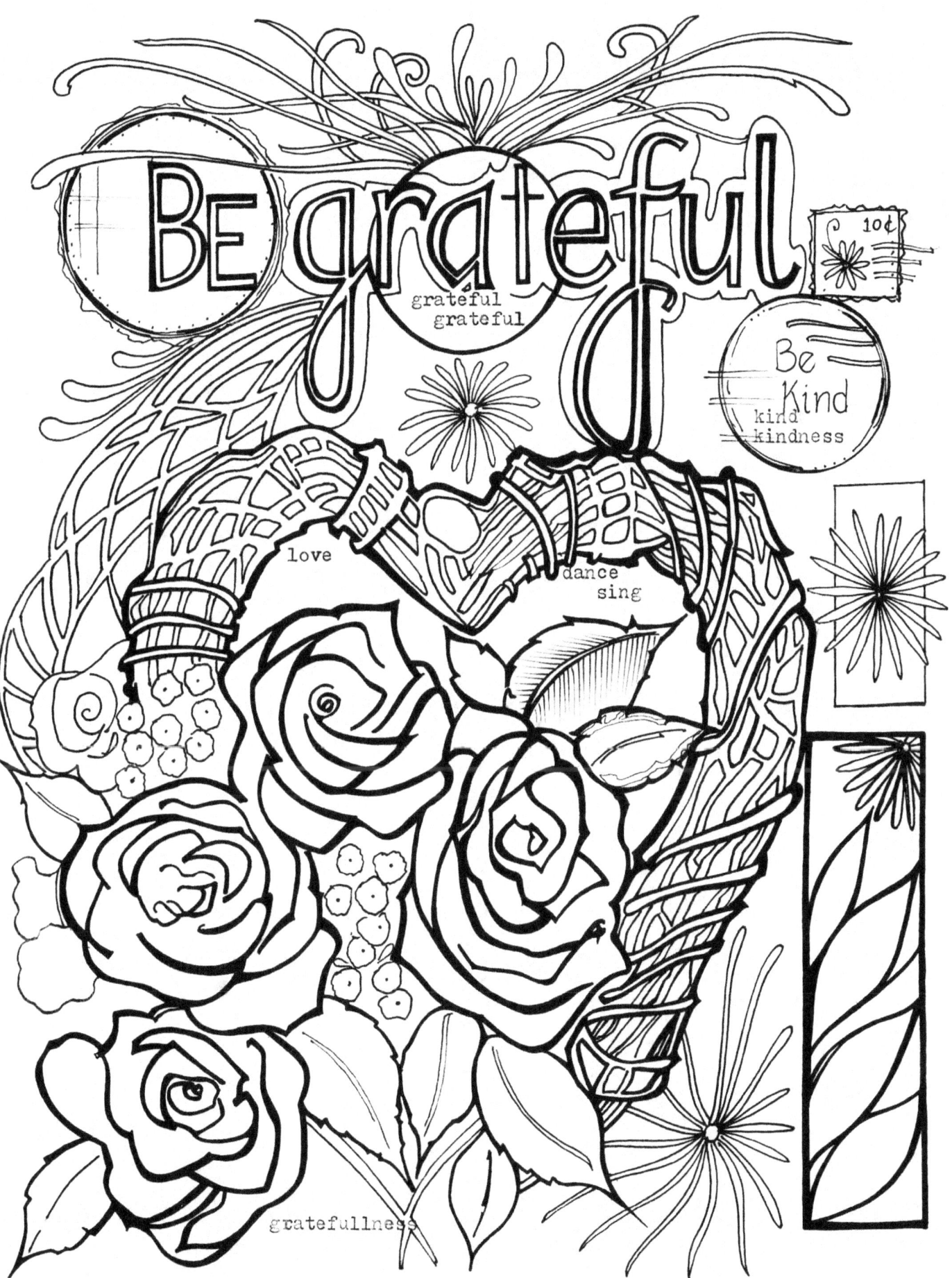

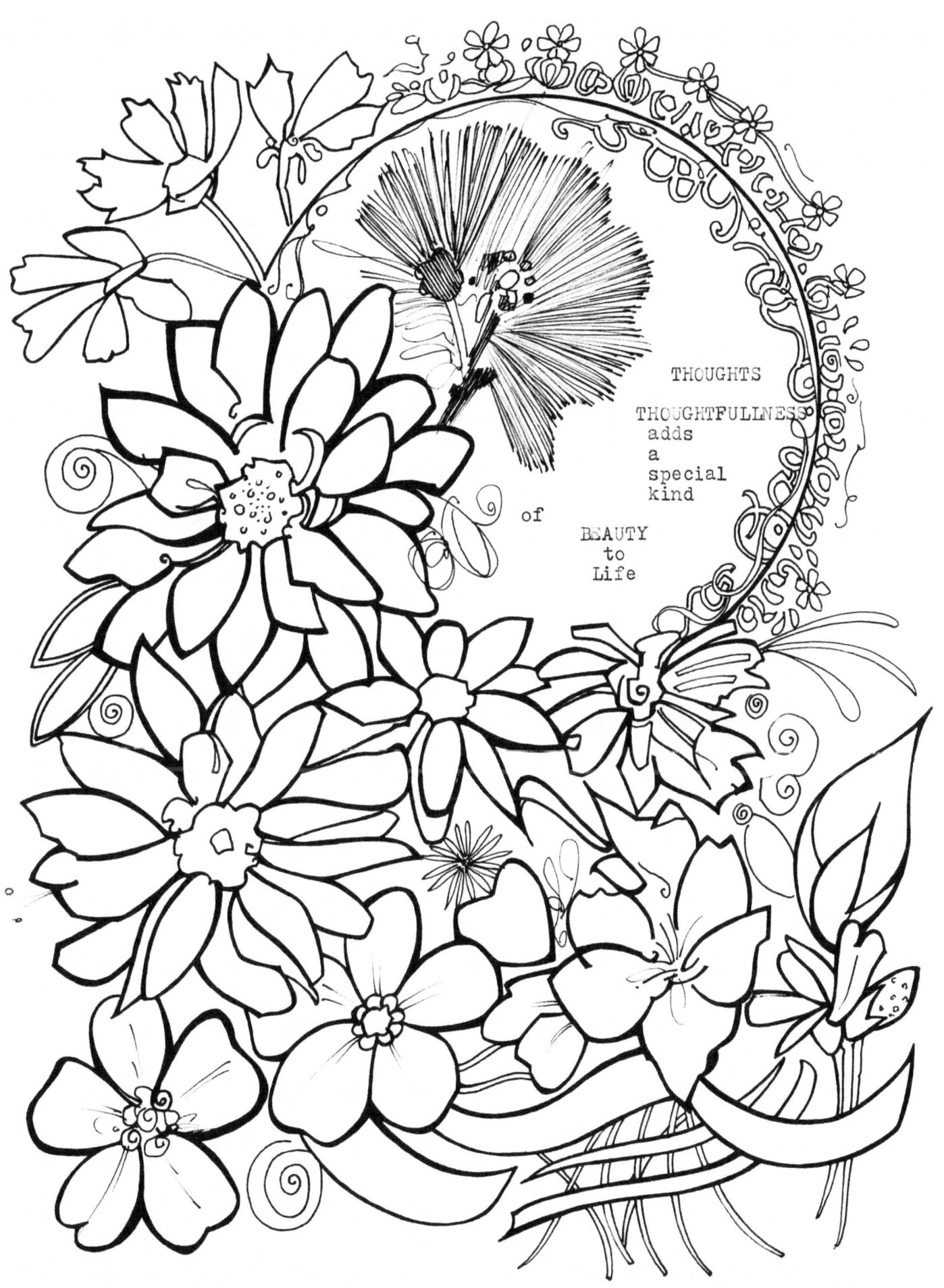

THOUGHTS

THOUGHTFULLNESS
adds
a
special
kind

of

BEAUTY
to
Life

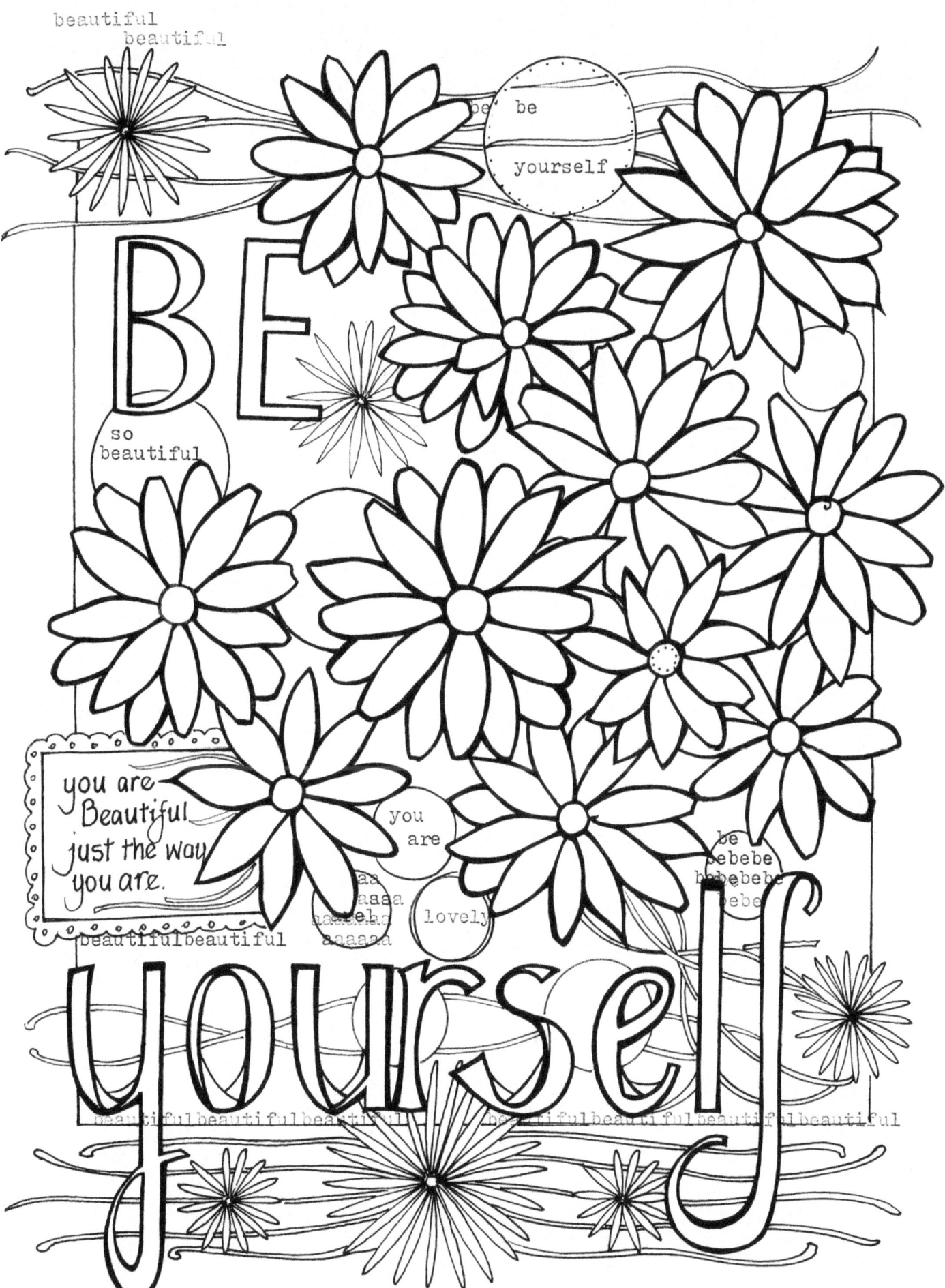

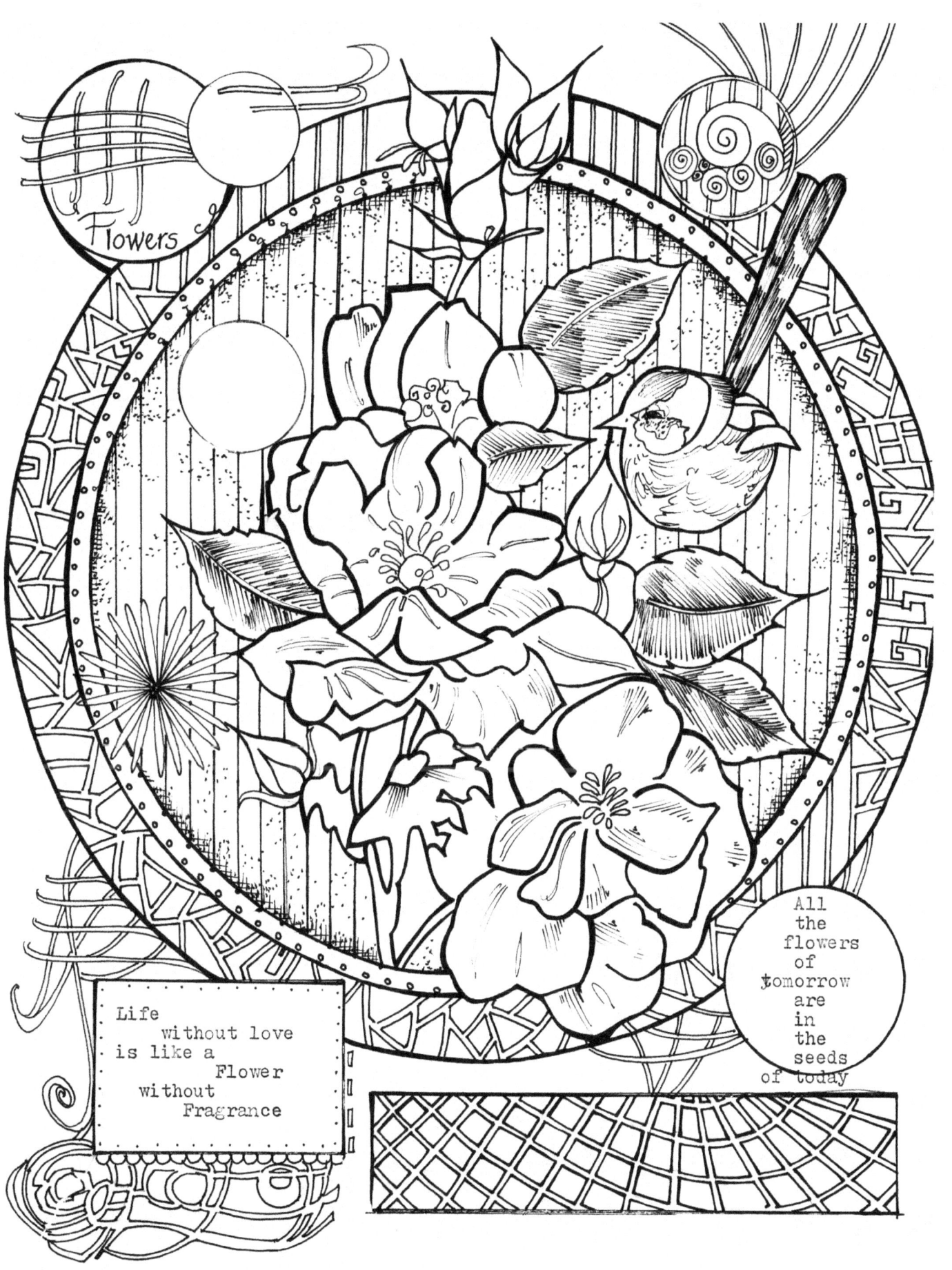

Flowers

Life
    without love
is like a
        Flower
without
    Fragrance

All
the
flowers
of
tomorrow
are
in
the
seeds
of today

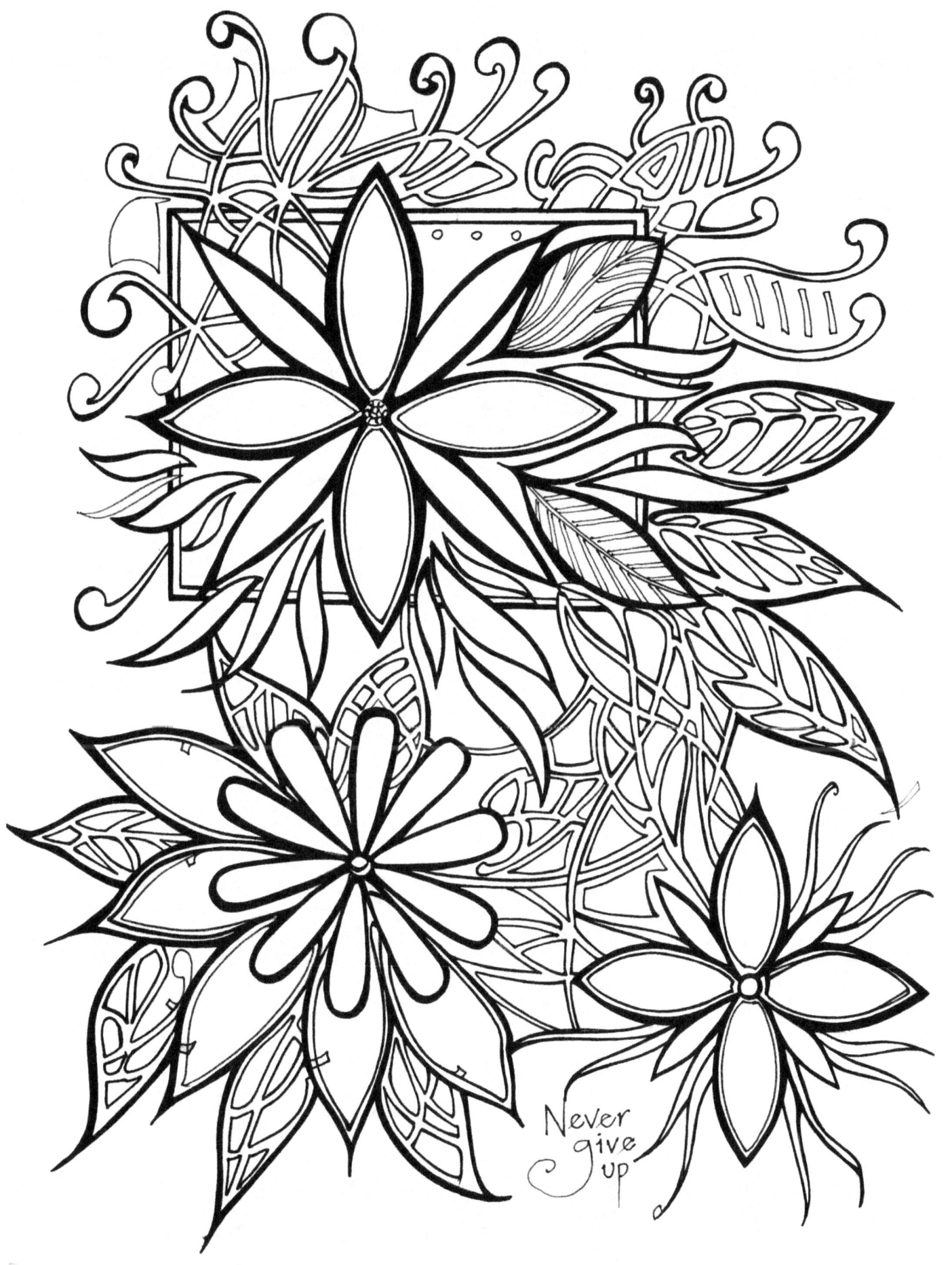

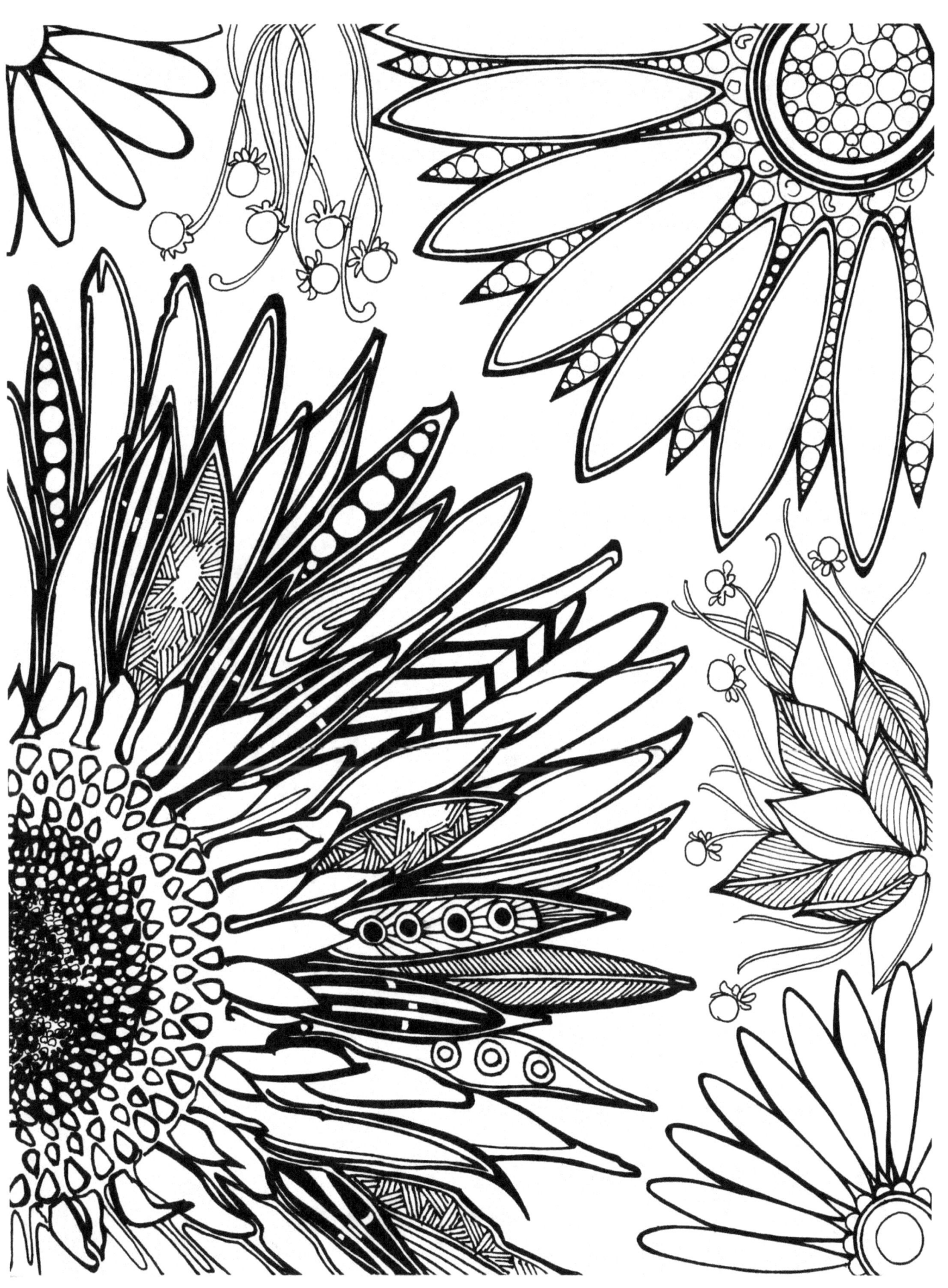

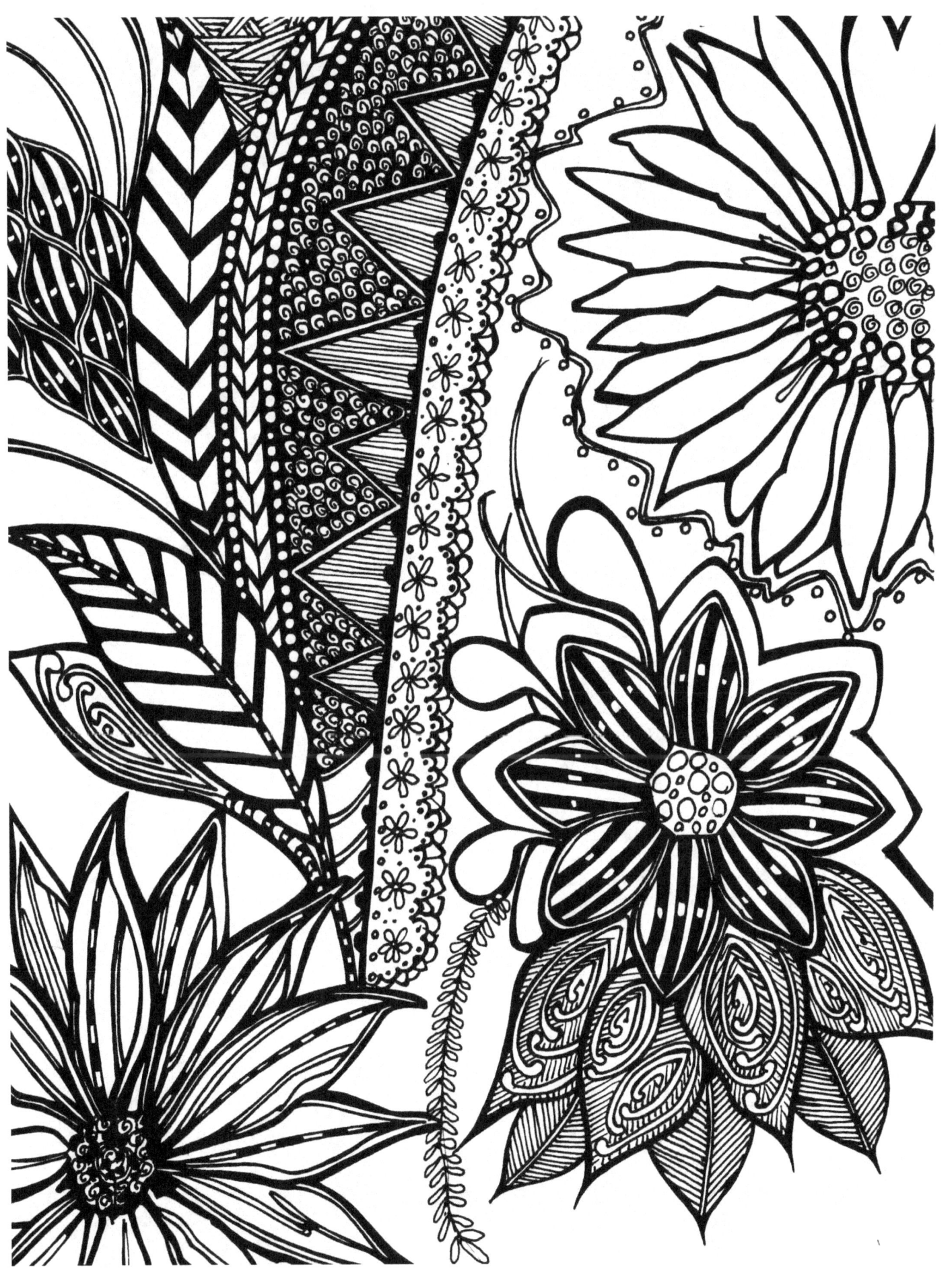

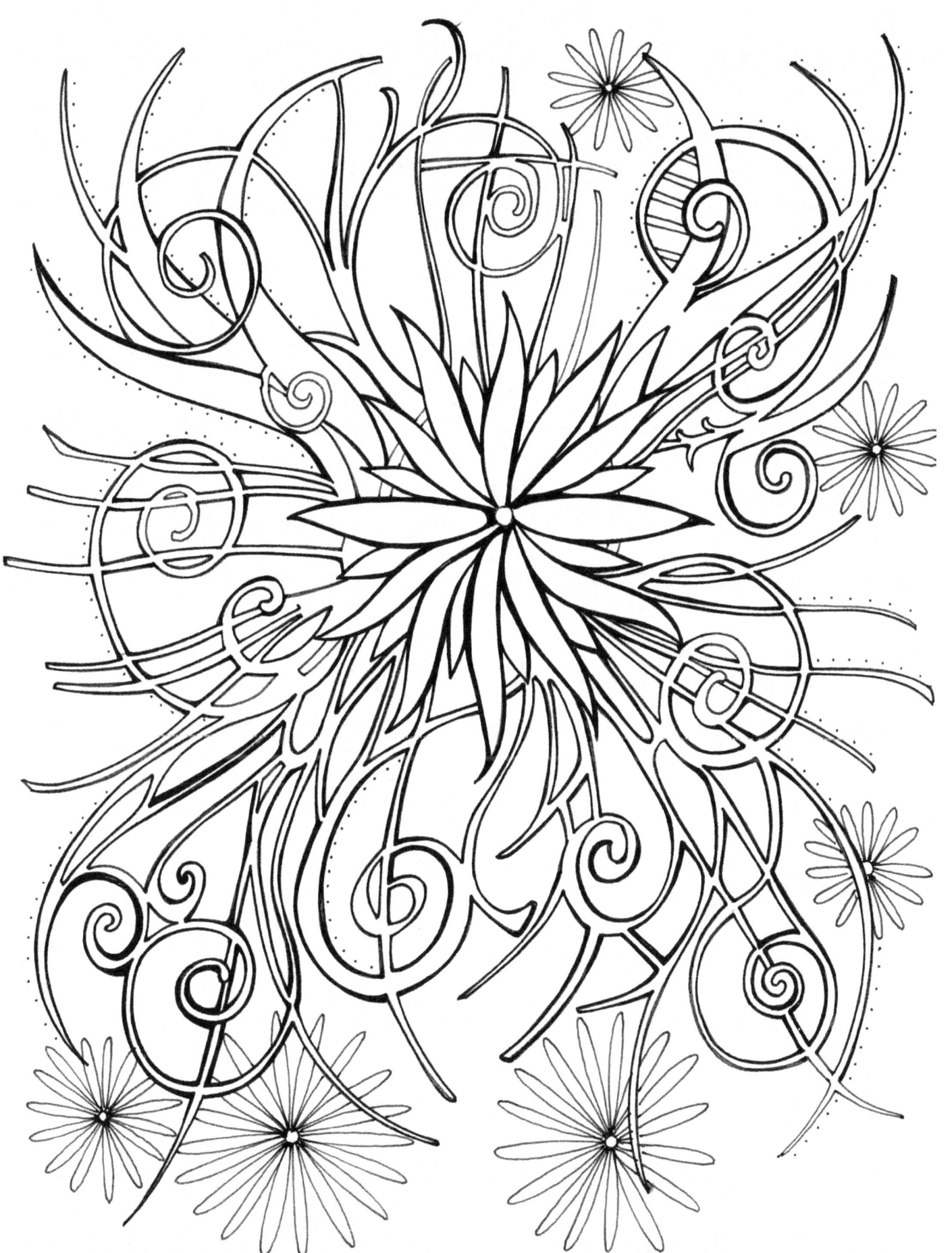

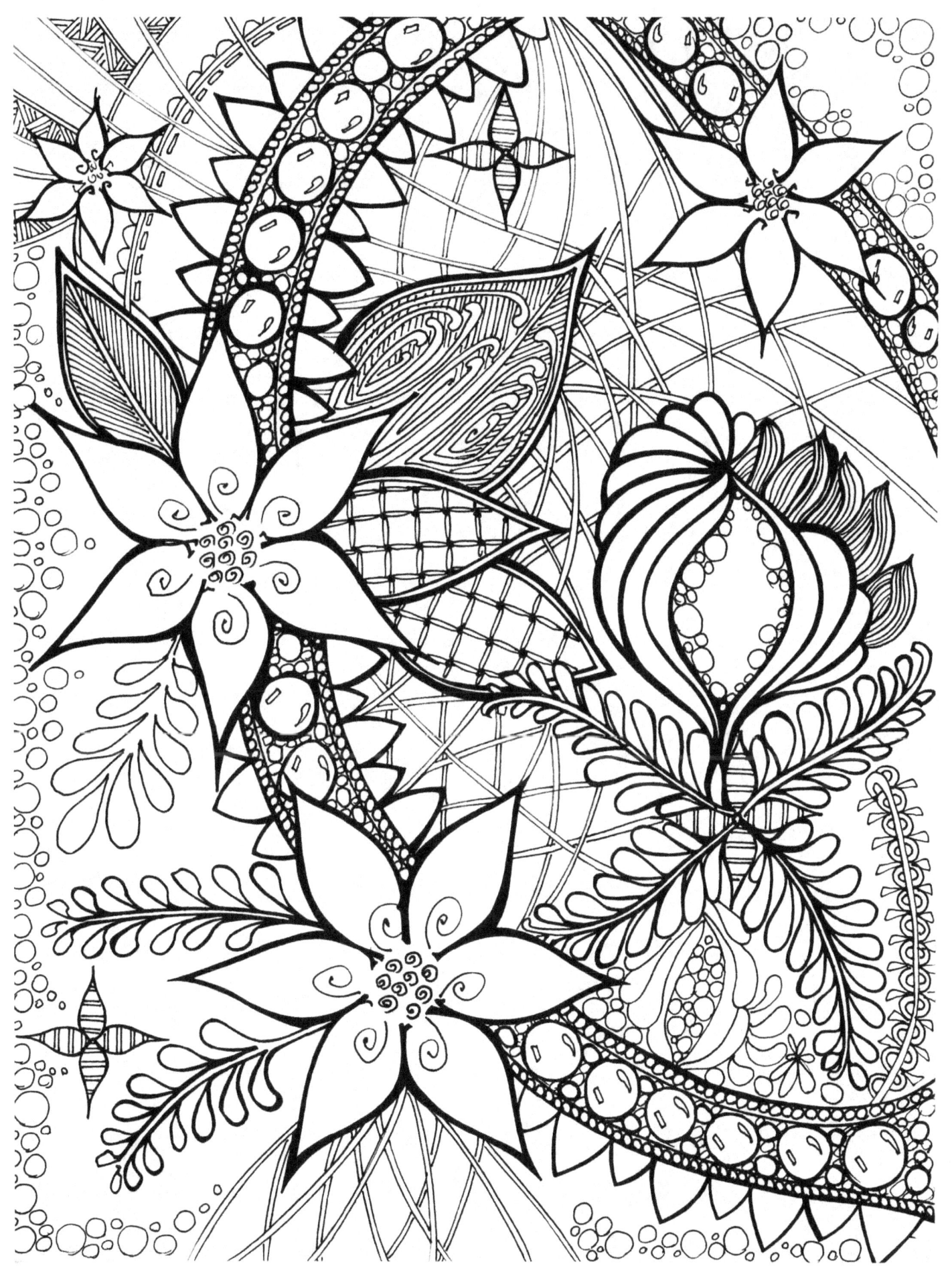

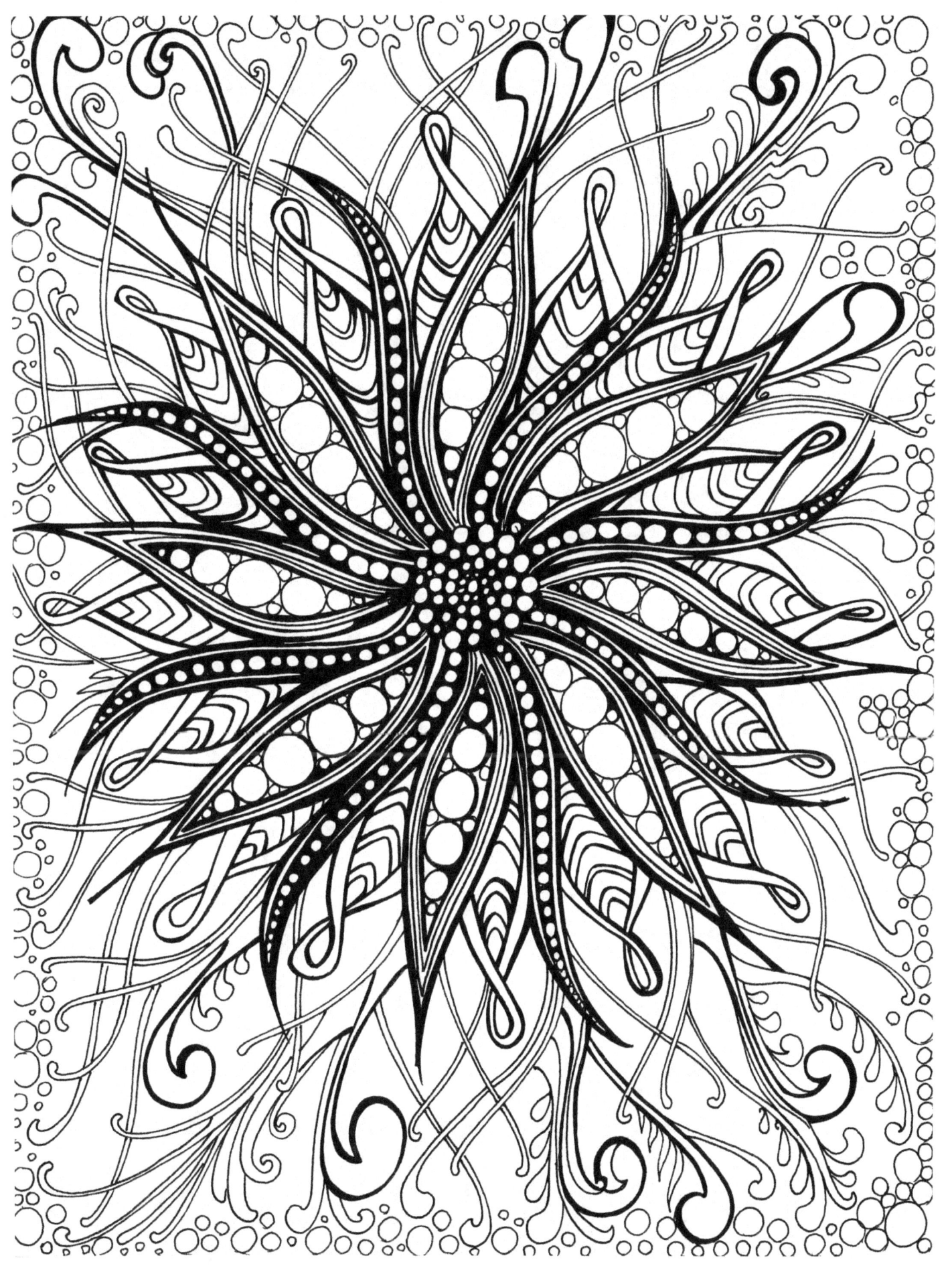

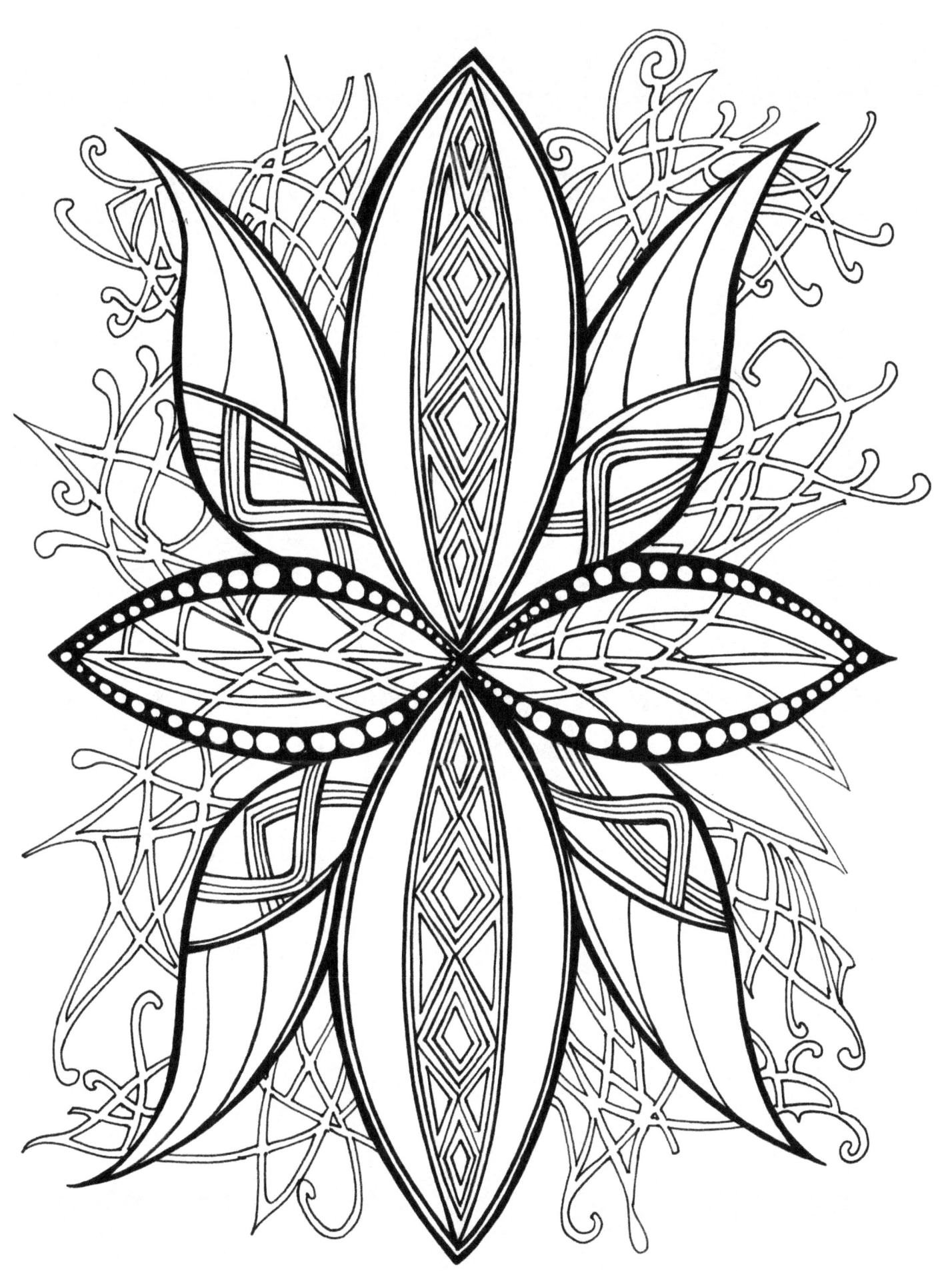

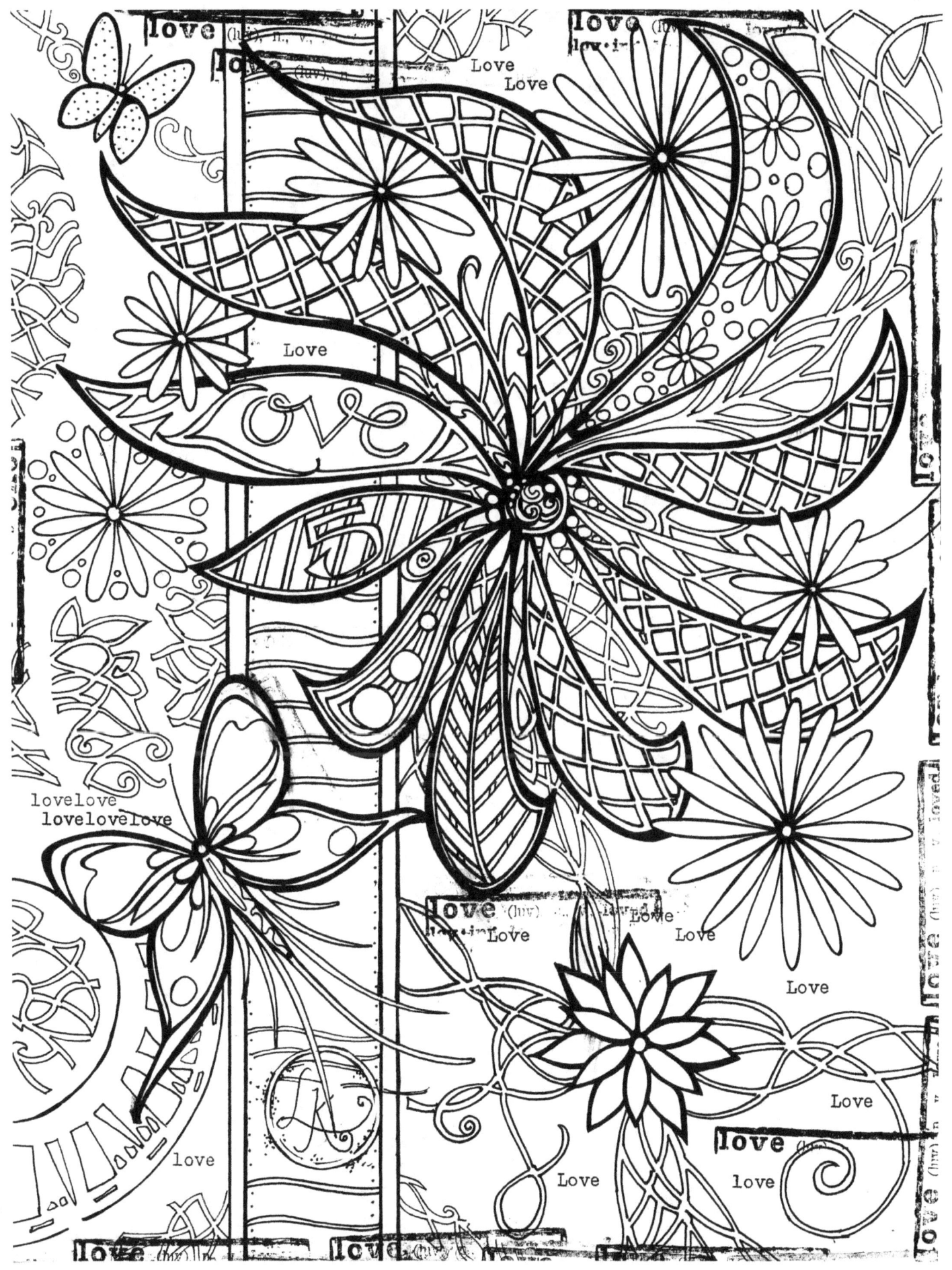

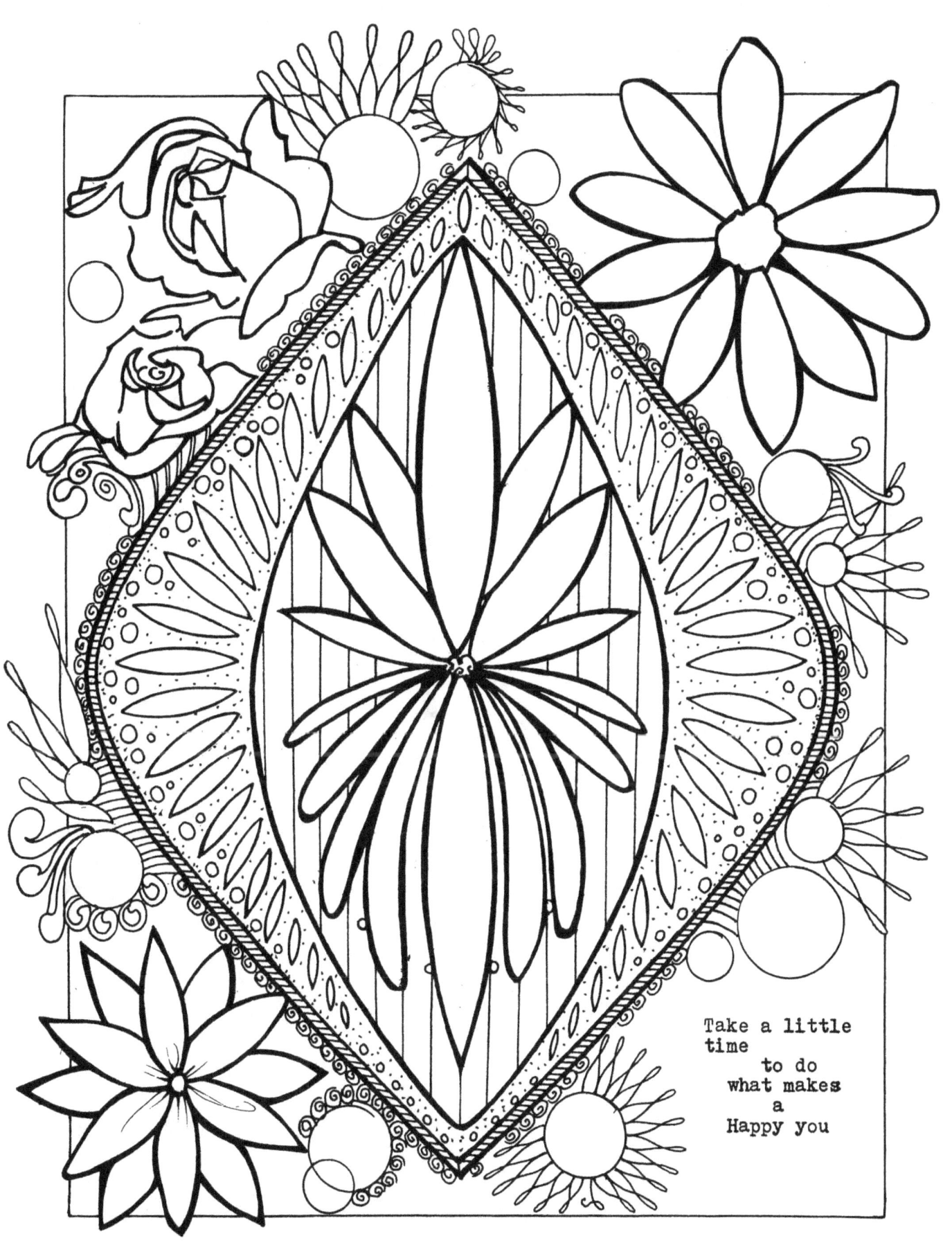

Take a little
time
   to do
what makes
   a
Happy you

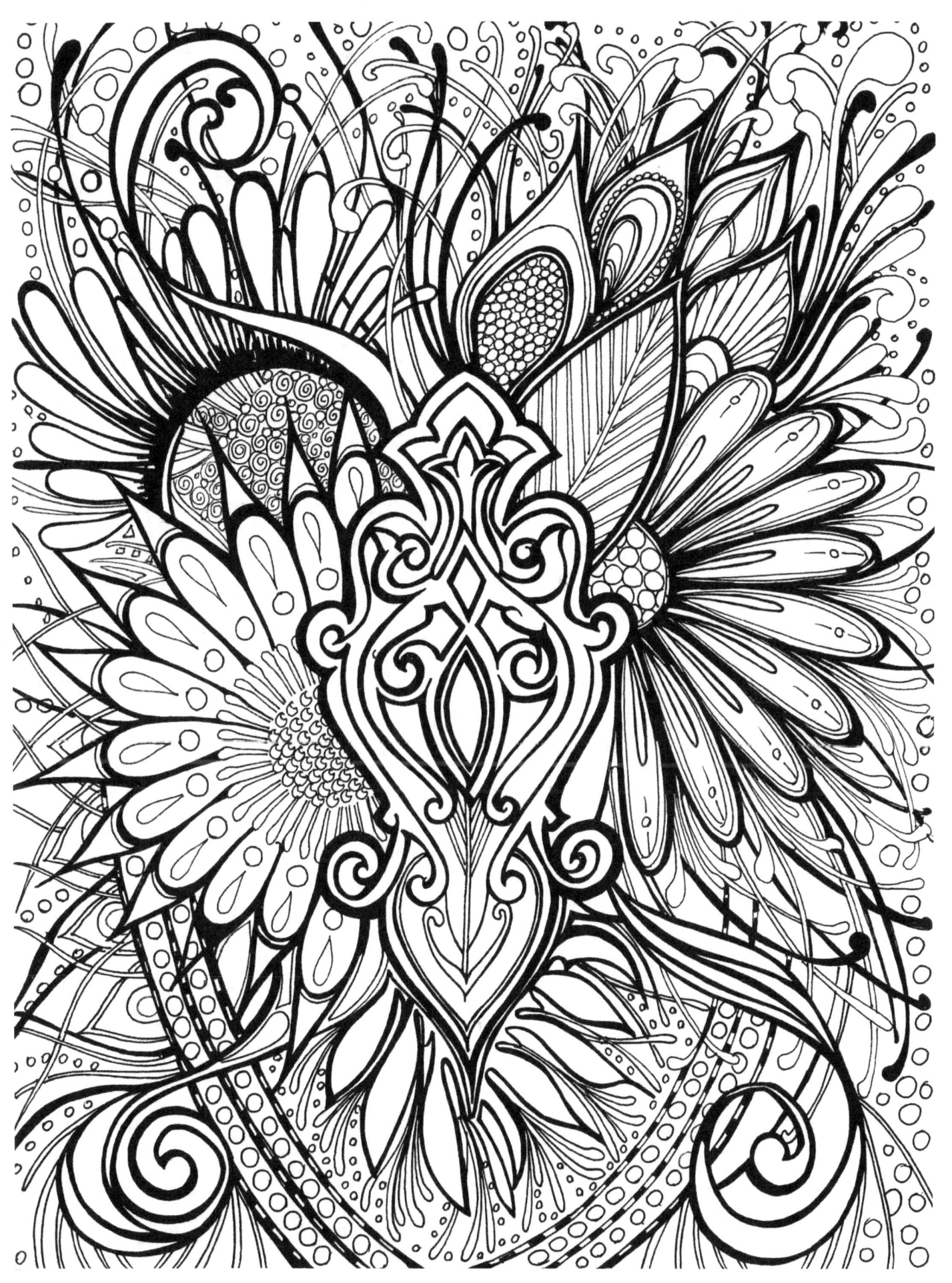

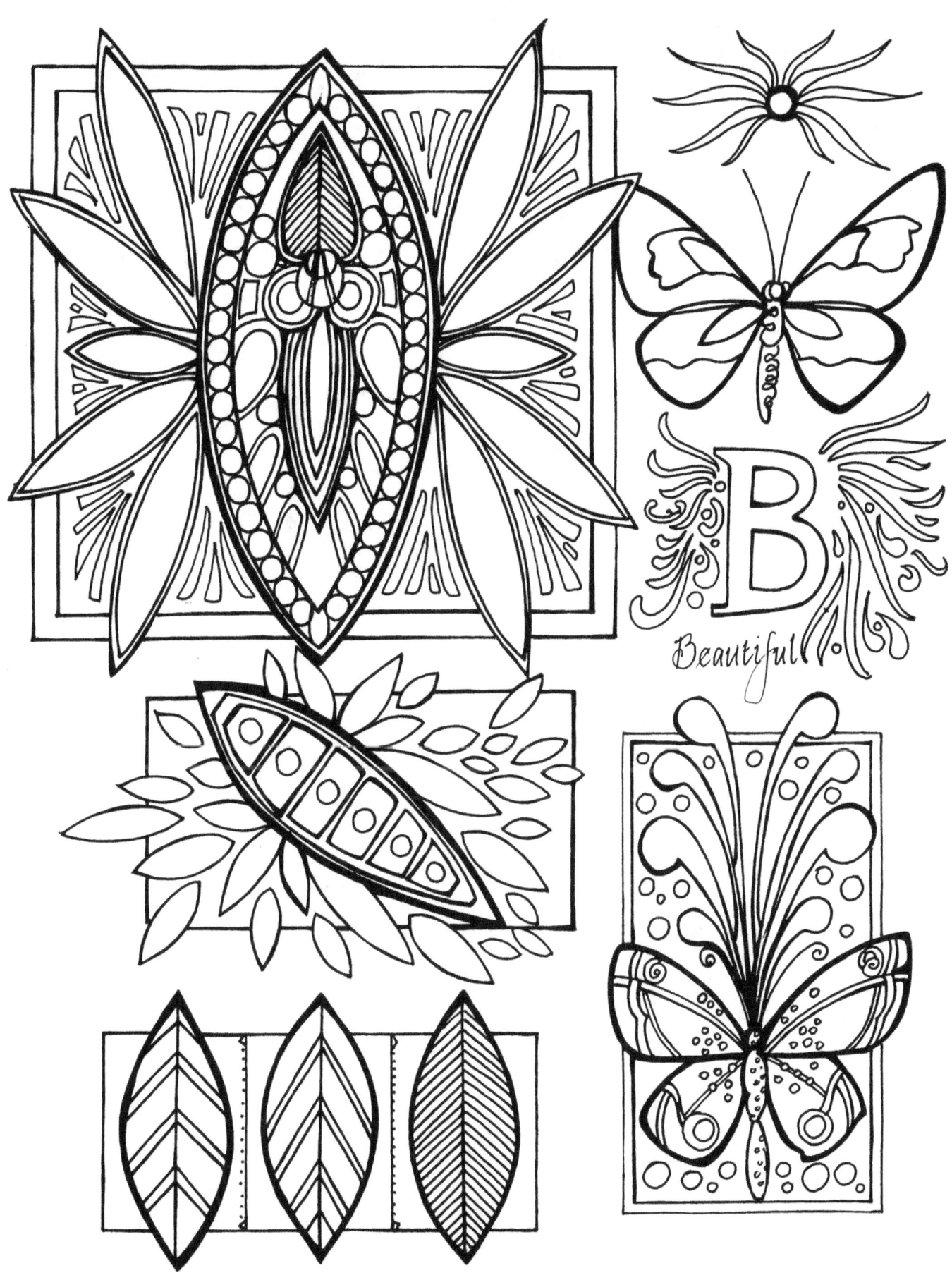

B

Beautiful

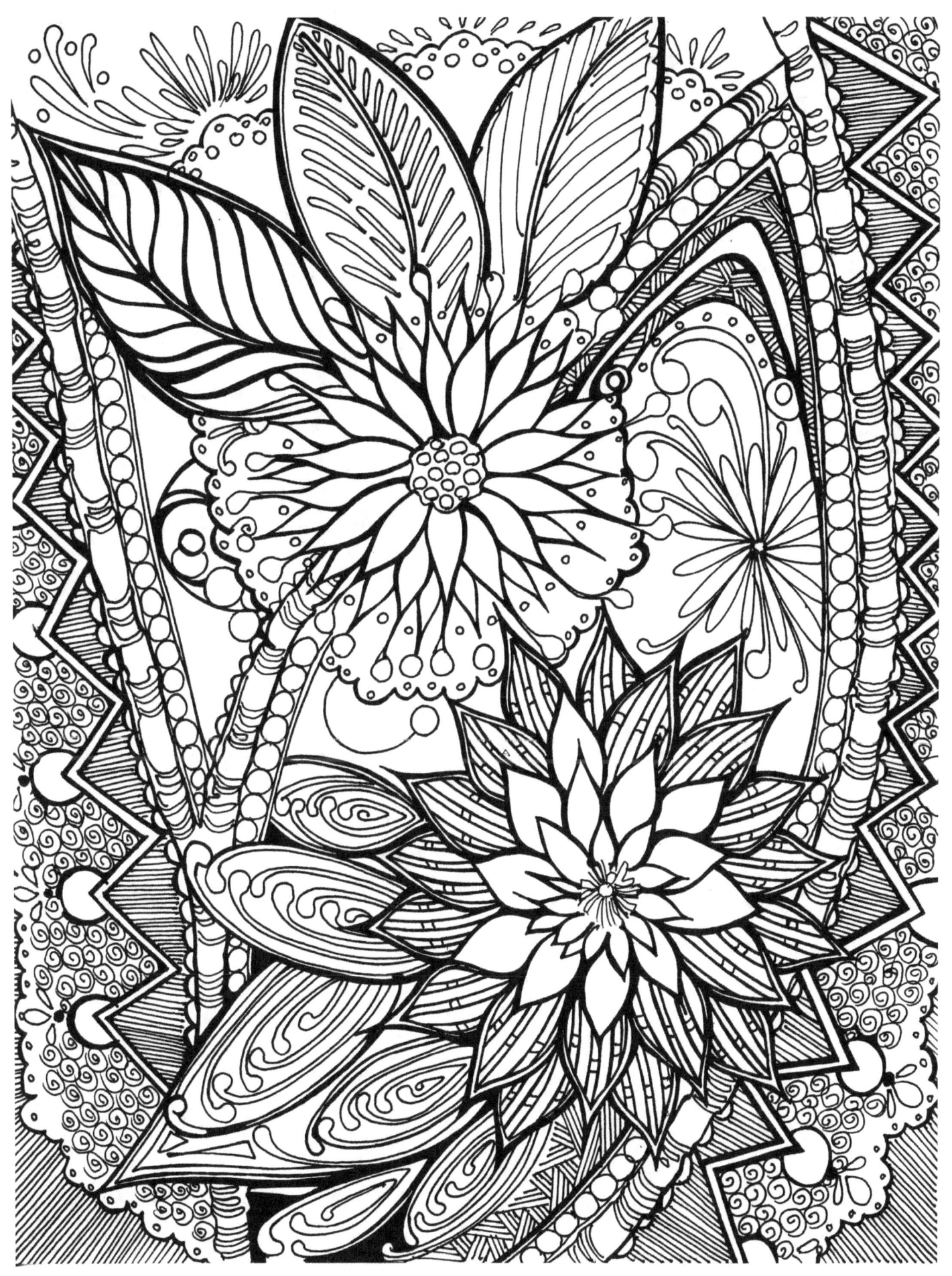

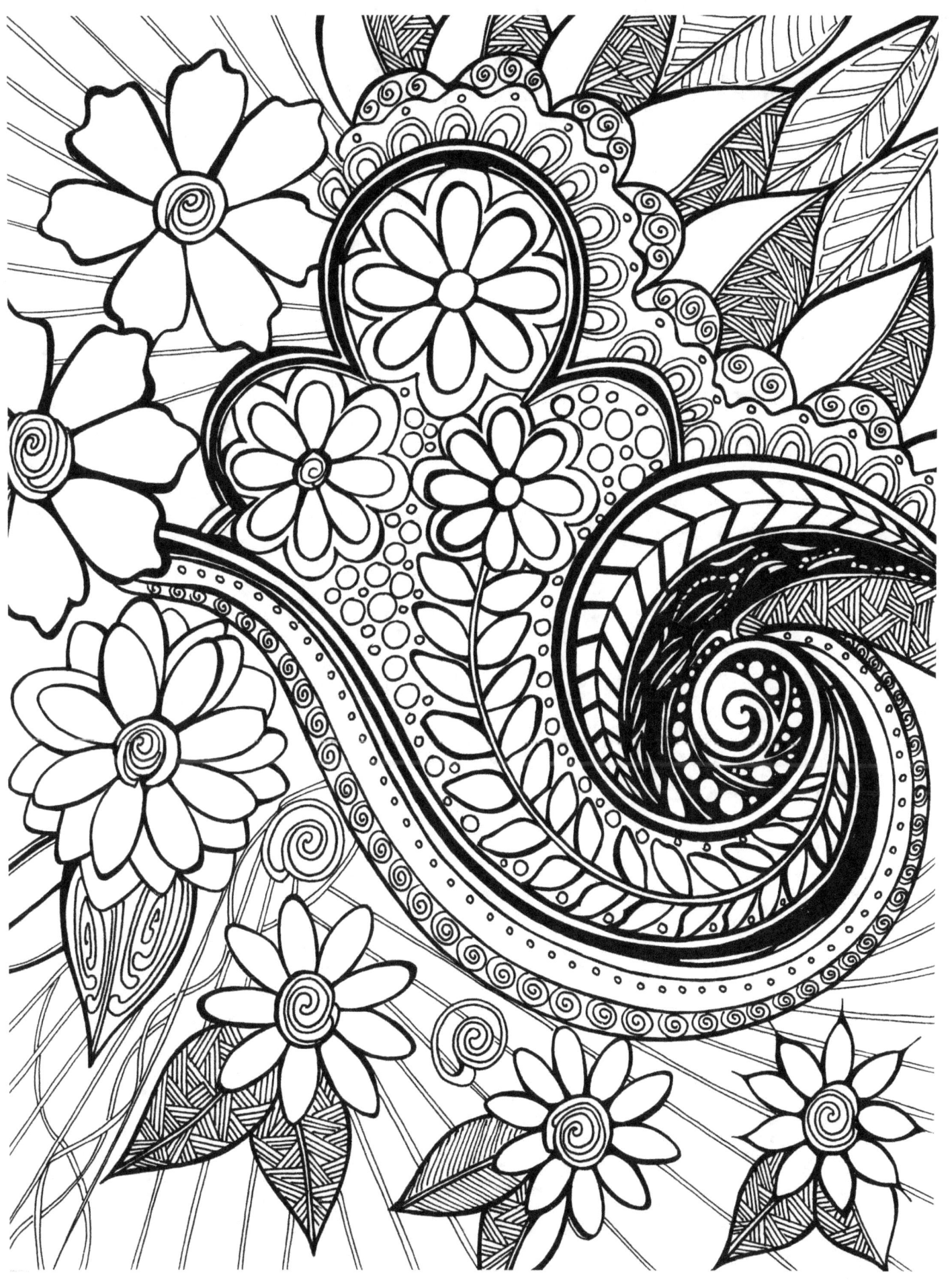

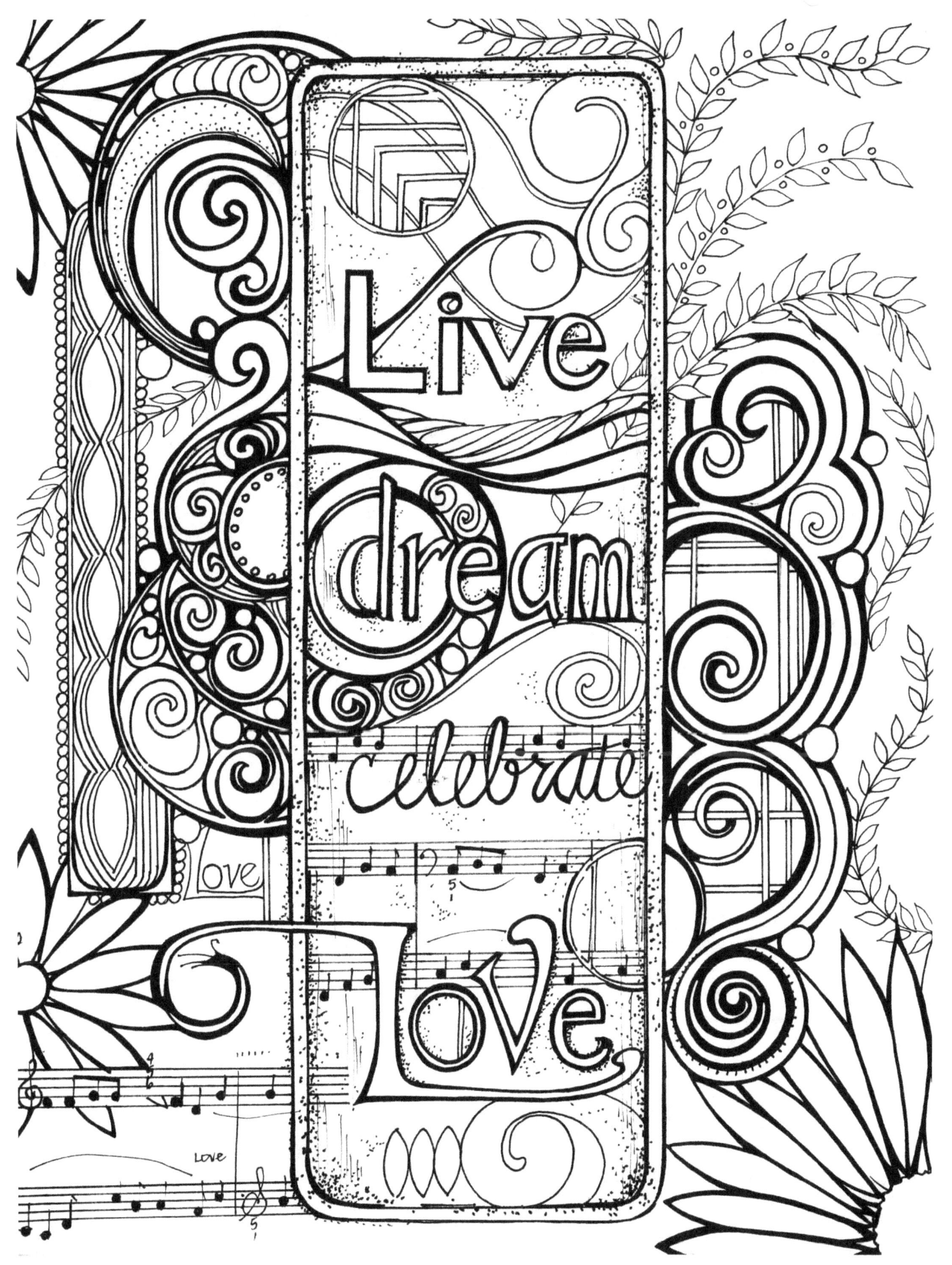

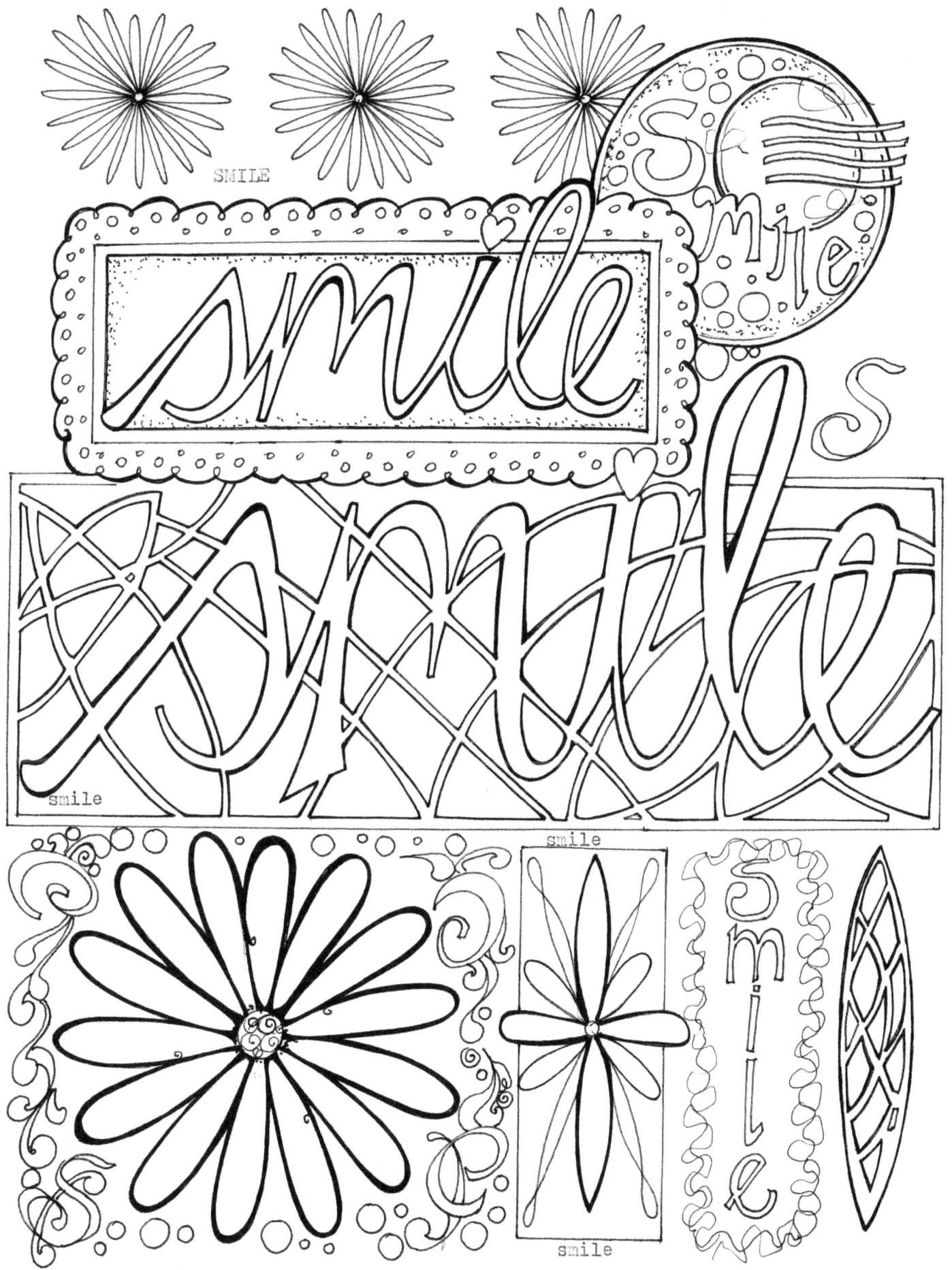

www.ingramcontent.com/pod-product-compliance
Lightning Source LLC
Chambersburg PA
CBHW060012210526
45170CB00017B/2313